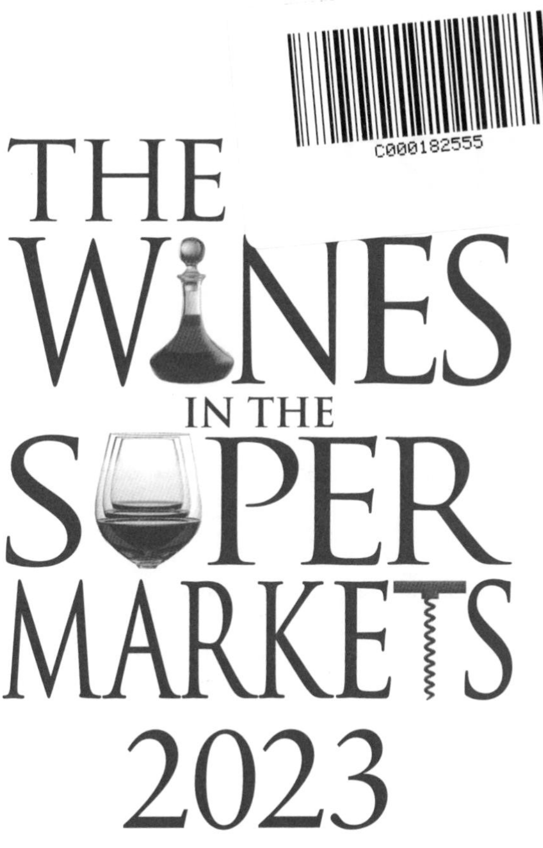

THE WINES IN THE SUPERMARKETS 2023

NED HALLEY

foulsham
LONDON • NEW YORK • TORONTO • SYDNEY

W. Foulsham & Co. Ltd
for Foulsham Publishing Ltd
The Old Barrel Store, Drayman's Lane, Marlow, Bucks SL7 2FF

Foulsham books can be found in all good bookshops and direct from www.foulsham.com

ISBN: 978-0-572-04828-0

A CIP record for this book is available from the British Library

Printed and bound in Great Britain by Martins the Printers Ltd

Contents

What price a glass of wine?

Tommy Cooper had it right. Short-changed in a pub, he eyeballed the barman and told him, 'it's not the principle, it's the money'.

If you like your wine as much as the great comedian liked his, you won't want discussions about the cost-of-living crisis, or how you choose to spend what little cash you have. You want to get your money's worth.

Readers of this book, I'm fairly convinced, will regard wine not as a luxury but as a necessity. Something we don't choose to do without. So as the global economy melts down and our consumer choice is curtailed, where to turn?

Welcome to *The Best Wines in the Supermarkets 2023*. It's the 18th successive annual edition and it is, as ever, dedicated to the cause of finding delicious, restorative wines at the most advantageous prices. Now I fully realise that the supermarkets, along with petrol stations, railway operators, energy companies and the rest, are suspected of ripping us all off with no thought to the common good. But consider this. Prices for wines on most retail multiples' shelves have hardly risen at all for several years. We might be in double-digit inflation, but wine, especially in supermarkets, is in price stasis.

It's odd, but it's not complicated. Worldwide production of wine exceeds demand, and has done for yonks. While supply grows and grows (everybody wants to be a winemaker), demand is continually diminished by health scares and belief-based prohibitions. And, of course, by lack of resources (poverty) and taxation. In Britain, we pay swingeing excise duty on all alcohol.

But we always have. And those who rule over us know that if they hike the impost too much they will encounter the law of diminishing returns. We'll drink less of the heavily taxed stuff and the overall revenue will fall. So wine is one of very few commodities not going up significantly in price. And here's the thing: quality is going up. Choose wisely from the growing ranges of own-label wines offered by the supermarkets and you can forget the horrible 'global' brands supported (and price-inflated) by advertising campaigns.

This book does not concern itself with these brands or any other kind of bad wine. My aim is to pinpoint quality at a rational price, and I believe the best source for this objective is a big supermarket. Not a corner shop or convenience store. A proper chain supermarket.

In spring/summer 2022 I have had the honour of invitations to taste new and new-vintage wines from the Co-op, Majestic, Marks & Spencer, Tesco and Waitrose. It was wonderful to try so many interesting wines at the retailers' expense for the first time since 2019. Well, Tesco excepted. See the Tesco entry for the full, tragic story.

I found out too late that Aldi and Morrisons had put on tastings for the first time since the Covid all-clear, but neither of them invited me. Thanks a bunch, Aldi and Morrisons. As to Lidl, not a word, and I don't care. If Asda or Sainsbury's had tastings, they certainly didn't tell me.

So, I bought a few wines from Aldi, rather more at Morrisons and no more than absolutely necessary at Lidl. And I made a couple of visits to my nearest Asda and Sainsbury's stores to pick up some likely candidates at the most generous promotional prices I could find.

One consequence of the unevenness of my tasting opportunities is a certain unevenness of coverage in this edition. There are, you won't be surprised to learn, lots of wines from the Co-op, Majestic, Marks & Spencer and Waitrose. Quite a lot from Tesco and Morrisons, fewer from Aldi, Asda, Lidl and Sainsburys. But I am content that every wine in the book deserves its place and commend all of them with equal fervour.

Around the wine world, changing climate conditions, the continuing effects of Covid and of course the cost of living crisis, which was bad enough before Russia's war on Ukraine, have not done much to help the grape harvests of 2021–22 (depending on the hemisphere in which your vines are planted).

The European continent certainly had mixed fortunes in the vineyards. Wild weather was the principal problem. Severe late frosts cut harvests in some regions of France by as much as half. In Bordeaux, the freezes were bad enough, but mildew arising from warm, wet conditions reduced some yields even more. Champagne was also badly struck both by frosts and mildew. Freakish sub-zero spring temperatures in Provence decimated rosé production, with the important Var area further devastated by a week-long wildfire just before harvest. The Loire Valley felt the frosts too, with yields in Sancerre down by as much as two-thirds. Other famous appellations were laid waste by summer hail storms.

Italy didn't fare much better, with yields nationwide down about ten per cent on 2020. Piedmont in the north suffered frosts, then hail, then drought. In Sicily, fearsome heatwaves did the damage. Spain and Portugal have, happily, reported fewer troubles, but one particular region of Germany, the Ahr valley, was horribly flooded. Numerous vineyards and wineries were damaged or even swept away.

In the 'New' world, 2021–22 has certainly had its troubles. California has been beset by wildfires for several years in succession, with the Napa Valley among the vineyard regions worst affected. Australia likewise, following years of drought across the wine regions, has suffered equally. While vineyards can be isolated from the spread of flames, smoke damage alone from bushfires can spoil harvests or even kill the vines. But for all these troubles, quality is consistently reported to be unaffected just about everywhere. Wine shortages are not predicted. There's no good reason to worry prices will significantly rise. Competition is simply too intense.

While market forces may not escalate wine prices for the near future, however, taxation looks like it will. As Chancellor of the Exchequer, Rishi Sunak announced in his autumn budget of 2021 a set of proposed changes to alcohol duties that would make a clear impression on prices if implemented, possibly from February 2023. 'Our new system', Sunak announced, 'will be designed around a common-sense principle: the stronger the drink, the higher the rate. That's the right thing to do and it will help end the era of cheap, high-strength drinks which can harm public health and enable problem drinking'.

For wine drinkers, it would mean that only the alcohol level will determine the duty. The current extra duty on sparkling wines will be scrubbed. All wines of 11% abv upwards will be dutied on a rising scale. Industry body the Wine & Spirit Trade Association has estimated that the scheme would add about 10p to the duty on a bottle of still wine at 12% and about 58p to a 15% still wine. On a 12% sparkling wine duty drops about 50p and on a 17% fortified wine it rises about 32p. Turmoil in Westminster in autumn 2022 has meant these proposed measures are still up in the air as we go to press with this edition, but should they be implemented they could have real impact on retail prices.

Would the wine trade try to absorb these higher impositions for fear of losing sales? Obviously the sparkling wine sector is on to a winner, but I can't see the prices of champagne, prosecco and the rest taking much of a dip. Maybe the extra margins earned could balance out the costs to the still-wine sector. We'll just have to wait and see.

Let us not end on this uncertain note, but pause a moment to reflect on another prospect for 2023. This momentous year happens to be the 75th anniversary of the British supermarket. It all started, we are told, in January 1948, when the London Co-operative Society opened its first self-service shop in the East End of the metropolis. The word supermarket, according to the Oxford English dictionaries, had been adopted a decade earlier from American English, five years after its first recorded use in the United States.

In Britain, supermarkets have been the dominant force in grocery retailing as long as any of us can remember, but they have been licensed to sell alcohol only since 1962. By 1972 they had 25 per cent of the retail beer, wine and spirits market. Now it's more like 70 per cent. Supermarkets sell about £13 billion worth of alcohol a year including £6 billion of wine.

They've taken over the everyday wine business. Just like that.

Fit to drink?

I have much appreciated a report in the journal *Frontiers of Nutrition* of a study during the Covid-19 epidemic 2020–2022. Based on data from the medical records of 474,000 Britons, researchers tracked the relationship between moderate alcohol-consumption and Covid infection. Compared to the infection rate among total abstainers, the risk to red-wine drinkers was 10 to 17 per cent lower, and to white and sparkling wine drinkers 7 to 8 per cent lower. The news for beer and cider drinkers was less good. They face a 28 per cent higher risk of Covid-19 infection than non-drinkers.

Where does the best wine come from?

It's France, I suppose. Fabled estates in Bordeaux, Burgundy and Champagne have a perpetual monopoly on the most-venerated red, white and sparkling wines, worldwide. If your budget per bottle starts at £100 I guess that's all you need to know. But for those of us who buy wine in supermarkets and consider even £10 a bit of a punt, the question needs to be readdressed.

In the global context, you could argue that the country of origin of any wine is immaterial. But the supermarkets wouldn't agree with you. They arrange all the wines in their stores and on their websites precisely according to their nationality.

It's quite odd. You wouldn't display your canned fruits and vegetables this way, would you? Or your frozen fish? Or anything else, really? But that's the way they do the wine and, accordingly, that's the way I arrange the listings in this book.

To be fair, the wines of particular nations and regions do have identifiable attributes even when made from a common grape variety. The white wines from fashionable Sauvignon Blanc, for example, have distinct styles at home in France's Loire Valley and away in the Marlborough region of New Zealand. Chilean Sauvignon has its own qualities, and so does South African.

Germany, though never in fashion, makes inimitably delicious wines from the Riesling grape. Australian wines from this noble variety are so different that I suspect uninitiated devotees of the Mosel and Rhine would hardly recognise a Clare Valley Riesling at all.

While the grape does much to determine the nature of the wine, location still counts for a lot. Landscape and soil conditions, weather and the peculiar skills and customs of the winemakers all have their parts to play.

The French have a word for it: *terroir*, which loosely translates as 'soil', but *vignerons* in France take it to mean the entirety of conditions local to the site of crop production. That's not just the soil but the lie of the land, its geographical position, its climate and indeed what the tillers of that soil and the custodians of the crops get up to.

On visits to France, I have heard much of terroir. Amid the most-valued vineyards of Chablis I have learned that the ground is composed largely of oyster shells, mountainised over millennia into vertiginous slopes. From these bleak, frost-ravaged heights come some of the world's most minerally luscious dry white wines. I've had it all endlessly explained to me and never really understood, but be in no doubt: *grand cru* Chablis is like no other wine.

And so on across all of France. Elsewhere, winemakers might not speak of terroir, but they all believe in the real or imagined unique properties of their estates. They all consider their wines to be an expression of their locations and traditions. This is what gives wine its much-treasured diversity, and of course its mystique. Wine is more than a mere nutritious drug. It's part natural phenomenon, part art form. Hurrah to that, I say.

It's all about the grape variety

The grape, naturally, counts for everything in wine. The finished product is, after all, simply the fermented juice of the fruit. Well, yes, there will be a cultured yeast introduced to assist the process. And there are permitted additives, mostly sulphur products and clarifying agents, to ensure healthy, bright wine. The wine's natural sugars and acids can be supplemented.

But the grape variety still sets the pace. Dark-skinned grapes make red wine because the skins are included in the must (pressed juice) during fermentation and give the wine its colour. The juice of virtually all grapes is clear. You can make white wine with dark-skinned grapes by extracting the juice promptly and fermenting it free of the skins. The base wine for Champagne is made largely from dark-skinned grapes. But still white wine is made much more simply – from pale-skinned grapes fermented without their skins.

Different grape varieties produce correspondingly different wines. There are hundreds of distinct varieties, but a couple of dozen account for most production. All of us have favourites, or at least preferences. The varieties described here account for most of the wines on offer in the supermarkets.

Red wine varieties

Aglianico: Ancient variety of southern Italy said to have been imported by immigrant Greek farmers around 500 BC. The name is a recent rendering of former Ellenico ('Hellenic') and the grape has caught on again thanks to Aglianico del Vulture, a volcanic DOC of Basilicata. The wines are dark, intense, pungent and long-lived.

Barbera: The most widely planted dark-skinned grape of Piedmont in northwest Italy makes easy-drinking purple vigorous rasping red wine to enjoy young and also, increasingly, a darker, denser but still vigorous style given gravitas through oak-ageing. Mostly sold under denominations Barbera d'Asti and Barbera d'Alba. Unrelated to Barbaresco, a Piedmontese wine made from Nebbiolo grapes.

Cabernet Sauvignon: Originally of Bordeaux and the mainstay of claret, Cabernet berries are compact and thick-skinned, making wine of intense flavour and gripping tannin. The grandest wines need decades to develop their full bloom. Everyday wines made worldwide typically have dense colour, purple in youth, aromas of blackcurrants and cedar wood ('cigar box') and firm, juicy-savoury fruit.

Gamay: It's the grape of Beaujolais. Colour can be purple with a blue note; nose evokes new-squashed raspberries with perhaps a pear drop or two, the effect of carbonic maceration, the Beaujolais method of vinification. Fruit flavours are juicy, bouncing, even refreshing.

Grenache: The French name for the Garnacha, originally of Spain, where it is much employed in Rioja and other classic regions. HQ in France is the southern Rhône Valley with further widespread plantings across the country's

Mediterranean regions. Wines can be light in colour but emphatic in flavour with a wild, hedgerow-fruit style lifted with spice and pepper. Widely cultivated across the New World.

Malbec: The signature grape of Argentina. A native of Bordeaux, where it plays a minor blending role, it thrives in the high-altitude vineyards of Mendoza, a province of the Andean foothills. The best wines have dark colour and a perfume sometimes fancifully said to evoke leather and liquorice; flavours embrace briary black fruits with suggestions of bitter chocolate, plum and spice.

Merlot: Bordeaux variety very often partnering Cabernet Sauvignon in claret blends and also solo in fabled Pomerol wines including Château Petrus. The grape is large and thin-skinned compared to Cabernet, making wine of rich ruby colour with scents evoking black cherry and cassis and fruit that can be round and rich. Ordinary wines are soft, mellow and early developing but might lack the firmness of tannin that gives balance.

Pinot Noir: It's the solo grape of proper red burgundy and one of three varieties in champagne. Everyday Pinot wines typically have a bright, translucent ruby colour and aromas evoking red soft summer fruits and cherries. Flavours correspond. Fine Pinot has elegant weight and shape, mysteriously alluring. New Zealand makes distinctive, delicious, sinewy Pinots; Chile produces robust and earthy Pinots; California's best Pinots compare for quality with fabulously expensive Burgundies.

Sangiovese: The grape of Chianti, so-named after the Latin for 'the blood of Jove', makes pleasingly weighted, attractively coloured wines with plummy perfume, even pruny in older wines, and slinky flavours evoking blackcurrant, raspberry and occasionally nectarine. Good Chianti always has a clear tannic edge, giving the wine its trademark nutskin-dry finish.

Syrah: At home in southern France, the Syrah makes wines that at their best are densely coloured, rich in aromas of sun-baked blackberries, silky in texture and plumply, darkly, spicily flavoured. The grandest pure-Syrah wines, such as Hermitage and Côte Rôtie, are gamey, ripe and rich and very long-lived. Syrah is widely planted across Mediterranean France as a blending grape in wines of the Côtes du Rhône and Languedoc. Under the name Shiraz, Syrah is Australia's most prolific red-wine variety.

Tempranillo: The grape at the heart of Rioja has to work hard. The unique selling point of the region's famous red wines is the long ageing process in oak casks that gives the finished product its creamy, vanilla richness – which can all too easily overwhelm the juiciness and freshness of the wine. The Tempranillo's bold blackcurranty-minty aromas and flavours stand up well to the test, and the grape's thick skin imparts handsome ruby colour that doesn't fade as well as firm tannins that keep the wine in shape even after many years in cask or bottle. Tempranillo is widely planted throughout Spain, and in Portugal, under numerous assumed names.

White wine varieties

Albariño: Rightly revered Iberian variety once better known in its Minho Valley, Portugal, manifestation as Alvarinho, a mainstay of vinho verde wine. Since the 1980s, Albariño from Spain's Galicia region, immediately north of Portugal, has been making aromatic and scintillatingly racy sea-fresh dry white wines from vineyards often planted close to the Atlantic shore. The seaside DO of

Rias Baixas, now a major centre for gastro-tourism, is the heart of Albariño country. The variety, characterized by small, thick-skinned berries with many pips, is now also cultivated in California, New Zealand and beyond.

Chardonnay: Universal variety still at its best at home in Burgundy for simple appley fresh dry wines all the way up to lavish new-oak-fermented deluxe appellations such as Meursault and Montrachet making ripe, complex, creamy-nutty and long-developing styles. Imitated in Australia and elsewhere with mixed success.

Chenin Blanc: Loire Valley variety cultivated for dry, sweet and sparkling white wines, some of them among France's finest. Honeyed aromas and zesty acidity equally characterize wines including elegant, mineral AOP Vouvray and opulent, golden late-harvested AOP Coteaux du Layon. In South Africa, Chenin Blanc now makes many fascinating and affordable wines.

Fiano: Revived southern Italian variety makes dry but nuanced wines of good colour with aromas of orchard fruit, almonds and candied apricots and finely balanced fresh flavours. Fleetingly fashionable and worth seeking out.

Glera: Widely planted in the Veneto region of northeast Italy, it's the principal variety in prosecco sparkling wine. The grape itself used to be named prosecco, after the winemaking village of Prosecco near Treviso, but under a 2009 change to the wine-denomination rules, the name can now be applied exclusively to the wine, not the grape. Glera makes a neutral base wine with plenty of acidity. It is a prolific variety, and needs to be. Sales of prosecco in Britain have now surpassed those of champagne.

Palomino Fino: The grape that makes sherry. The vines prosper in the *albariza*, the sandy, sun-bleached soil of Andalucia's Jerez region, providing a pale, bone-dry base wine ideally suited to the sherry process. All proper sherry of every hue is white wine from Palomino Fino. The region's other grape, the Pedro Ximenez, is used as a sweetening agent and to make esoteric sweet wines.

Pinot Grigio: At home in northeast Italy, it makes dry white wines of pale colour and frequently pale flavour too. The mass-market wines' popularity might owe much to their natural low acidity. The better wines are aromatic, fleetingly smoky and satisfyingly weighty in the manner of Pinot Gris made in the French province of Alsace. New Zealand Pinot Gris or Pinot Grigio follows the Alsace style.

Riesling: Native to Germany, it makes unique wines pale in colour with sharp-apple aromas and racy, sleek fruit whether dry or sweet according to labyrinthine local winemaking protocols. Top-quality Rhine and Mosel Rieslings age wonderfully, taking on golden hues and a fascinating 'petrolly' resonance. Antipodean Rieslings have more colour and weight often with a mineral, limey twang.

Sauvignon Blanc: Currently fashionable thanks to New Zealand's inspired adoption of the variety for assertive, peapod-nettle-seagrass styles. Indigenous Sauvignons from France's Loire Valley have rapidly caught up, making searingly fresh wines at all levels from generic Touraine up to high-fallutin' Sancerre. Delicate, elegant Bordeaux Sauvignon is currently on top form too.

Semillon: Along with Sauvignon Blanc, a key component of white Bordeaux, including late-harvested, golden sweet wines such as Sauternes. Even in dry wines, colour ranges up to rich yellow, aromas evoke tropical fruits and honeysuckle, exotic flavours lifted by citrus presence. Top Australian Semillons rank among the world's best.

Viognier: Formerly fashionable but perpetually interesting variety of the Rhône Valley makes white wines of pleasing colour with typical apricot aroma and almondy-orchardy fruit; styles from quite dry to fruitily plump.

More about these varieties and many others in 'A wine vocabulary' starting on page 122.

Brand awareness

Big-brand wines such as Blossom Hill and Hardy do not crowd the pages of this book. I do get to taste them, and leave most of them out. I believe they don't measure up for quality, interest or value.

The best wines in the supermarkets are very often own-brands. Own-brands date back to the 1970s, when interest in wine finally began to take root in Britain. Sainsbury's was first, with its own Claret, about 1975. It was hardly a revolutionary idea. Grand merchants like Berry Bros & Rudd (est 1698) had been doing own-label Bordeaux and much else besides, for ever.

In the supermarket sector, wine was bought on the wholesale market like anything else, from butter to washing powder. Only when interest in wine started to extend beyond the coterie served by the merchants did the mass retailers take any notice. It was thanks, of course, to the new craze for foreign travel, and to the good influence of writers like Elizabeth David, who revealed the joys of Continental-style food and drink. In 1966, Hugh Johnson's brilliant and accessible book *Wine* piqued the public consciousness as never before.

The adoption of supermarket wine was slow enough, but accelerated in the 1980s by the arrival of new, decent wines from Australia. Earlier on, cheap Aussie wines had been overripe, stewed rubbish, but breakthrough technology now enabled fresh, bold reds and whites of a different stripe. Wretched Europlonk brands like Hirondelle retreated before a tide of lush Chardonnay and 'upfront' Shiraz.

The horizon for supermarket wine buyers, always shackled by price constraint, was suddenly widened. In spite of the delivery distances, southern hemisphere producers could match their Old World counterparts for value as well as interest and quality.

In time, the winemakers of Europe fought back. Top estates carried on with 'fine wine' production, but humbler enterprises had to learn how to master real quality at the everyday level. They did. I believe the huge improvements in the simpler wines of the Continent owe much to the need to match the competition from the New World.

By the 1990s, Britain had become the world's biggest wine importer. Supermarkets were largely responsible, and now had muscle in the market. They started to dispatch their own people to vineyards and wineries worldwide, not just to buy the wines but to participate in their production. And always, they demanded the lowest-possible prices.

And so to today's proliferation of supermarket own-brands. They are the flagships of every one of the big grocers, and usually the focal point of promotions. They are, naturally enough, the wines of which their begetters are most proud. Mass-market brands do still persist in the supermarkets. Some are very good. I think of Blason, Chasse and Vieille Ferme from France; Baron de Ley and Miguel Torres from Spain; McGuigan and Penfolds from Australia; Catena from Argentina and Concha y Toro from Chile, among others.

If you have a favourite popular brand, do check the index to this book on page 156. It might not be mentioned in the entry for the supermarket where you're used to finding it, but that doesn't mean I've left it out.

Pick of the year

The honours are pleasingly well spread this year. A relatively modest 30 wines have won top scores compared to last year's enthusiastic 35 (I put my generosity down to Covid-linked sentimentality), shared out between no fewer than 12 producing nations.

There's one gong each for Argentina, Australia, Chile, Greece, Portugal and South Africa. Two apiece go to England, Germany and Romania. Spain gets three and France six. Italy triumphs with nine.

This is the first time in 18 successive editions of *The Best Wines in the Supermarkets* that France has not been the clear winner. Last year, 15 of the 35 gongs went to France, with Italy the runner-up on a mere 7.

What can it mean? Absolutely nothing as far as I'm concerned. It's just a bit of fun.

Among the favoured retailers, the honours are pretty even too. Waitrose is a predictable first with seven gongs, followed by M&S with a very creditable five. There are four apiece for the Co-op, Majestic and Tesco, three for Morrisons and two for Sainsbury's. One for Aldi and *nul points* for Lidl.

Yup. I think it sums up the year's comparative performances perfectly well.

Red wines

Wine	Retailer	Price
Vista Castelli Montepulciano d'Abruzzo 2020	Tesco	£4.75
Incanta Pinot Noir 2020	Majestic	£6.49
Taste the Difference Primitivo 2021	Sainsbury's	£7.00
Borgodei Trulli Salice Salentino 2020	Waitrose	£7.99
Waitrose Loved and Found Perricone 2020	Waitrose	£7.99
Robert Oatley Semaphore Cabernet Sauvignon 2018	Co-op	£8.00
Palladino Molise Biferno Riserva 2017	Co-op	£8.00
Vergelegen Cabernet Merlot Fairtrade 2019	Co-op	£9.00
Found Xinomavro Mandilaria 2020	M&S	£9.50
Château Recougne 2018	Majestic	£9.99
Mayu Titon Vineyard Syrah Gran Reserva 2017	Majestic	£9.99
Terre de Faiano Primitivo 2020	Waitrose	£9.99
Belpasso Vino Rosso 2019	Tesco	£10.00
Tilimuqui Organic Malbec 2021	Waitrose	£11.99

White wines

Morrisons Soave 2021	Morrisons	£4.85
Found Feteasca Regala 2021	M&S	£7.00
Found Ribolla Gialla 2021	M&S	£7.50
Bouchard Aîné et Fils Chardonnay Réserve du Conseiller 2020	Sainsbury's	£8.00
Waitrose Loved & Found Treixadura 2021	Waitrose	£8.99
Found Weiβburgunder 2021	M&S	£9.50
Wolfberger Alsace Pinot Blanc 2020	Waitrose	£10.99
The Best Chablis 2020	Morrisons	£15.00
Dr Hermann Ürziger Würzgarten Riesling Auslese 2006	Majestic	£16.99

Sparkling wines

Crémant de Jura 2019	Aldi	£8.49
Bramble Hill English Sparkling	M&S	£15.00
Balfour 1503 Foxwood Cuvee	Co-op	£17.50
Finest Premier Cru Champagne Brut	Tesco	£21.00

Fortified wines

Palo Cortado Sherry 37.5cl	Morrisons	£6.25
No 1 Torre del Oro Palo Cortado Sherry	Waitrose	£11.99
Finest Ten-Year-Old Tawny Port	Tesco	£12.50

Aldi

Short entry for the leading German discounter (Lidl trails far behind) this year. Aldi did stage a wine tasting for the media in 2022, but they didn't ask me, even though I had featured their wines on Channel 4's *Sunday Brunch* show. By the time I had heard of it, the tasting had been and gone.

Thanks a bunch, Aldi. I had missed the chance to try bold new introductions to the range including Chinese cabernet sauvignon, a £25 claret, a £30 burgundy, and assorted wines from Canada, Greece, England and Switzerland. Consequently, these bold innovations feature sparingly in the following pages.

The wines that do make it are either new vintages of bargains I have previously rated plus a few new wines I've bought in the stores. Range width varies wildly from branch to branch, but you can get most of these online if needs be.

My pick of the year from Aldi is a new moselle, Ockfener Bockstein Riesling Kabinett 2018 at just £6.49: a traditionally-made wine in its own right, and a predictor, I'd like to believe, that this German retailer might start offering us more of the produce of its own Fatherland.

RED WINES

ARGENTINA

9 **Buenas Vides Cabernet Sauvignon 2019** £5.99

Mendoza wine of sleekly developed blackcurranty style, well-balanced and ripe; 14.5% alcohol. Remarkable at this price.

8 **Specially Selected Buenas Vides Malbec 2020** £5.99

This Uco Valley generic seems to have been left over from last year – I reviewed it in the 2022 edition of this book – and I'm surprised as it has juicy blackberry charm as well as solid malbec heft; 14% alcohol. At the price, I'd certainly take a chance on the next vintage if it appears.

AUSTRALIA

9 **The Voyage Durif 2020** £7.99

This scored maximum points here in last year's guide, and Aldi is still listing it, but at £7.99 instead of £8.99. To reiterate: generous blackberry-pie savours, rustic spice, lovely weight and clean finish; 13.5% alcohol.

FRANCE

8 **Specially Selected Vacqueyras 2020** £11.99

Emboldened by a £9.99 promo offer, I risked this and came away impressed by the dark savours, spice and woof (14.5% alcohol) of this authentic product of a prestigious southern Rhône appellation, vigorous with hedgerow-fruit, sunny ripeness and satisfyingly complete.

PINK WINES

SPAIN

8 **Baron Amarillo Rioja Rosado 2021** **£6.99**

It does taste as you might expect: pink wine from the classic black-skinned grapes of the Rioja, briefly steeped with their skins pre-pressing to give the jolly party-frock-pink colour and fleeting berry fruit aromas amid the refreshingly crisp and balanced fruit; 13% alcohol.

WHITE WINES

ARGENTINA

8 **Buenas Vides Sauvignon Blanc 2021** **£5.49**

Grassy, brisk recognisable Latin sauvignon of easy charm at a price equally easy to like; 12.5% alcohol.

AUSTRIA

8 **Specially Selected Grüner Veltliner 2020** **£6.99**

This gently spicy aromatic example of Austria's flagship white wine is impressive at this price; 12.5% alcohol.

CANADA

8 **The Falls Canadian Riesling 2019** **£9.99**

You've got to give credit to Aldi for putting on this curiosity from the Great Lakes province of Ontario. It's comparable in style with both the German and the Australian styles of riesling, marrying crisp-apple raciness with grapey sweetness; 10.5% alcohol. A fine aperitif.

FRANCE

8 **Pierre Jaurant Côtes du Rhône Blanc 2020** **£6.49**

Brilliant to find the white wines of the southern Rhône infiltrating supermarket shelves. This bargain is well-coloured, peachily ripe and plump (13.5% alcohol) but brisk, lemon-tangy and refreshing into the bargain.

WHITE WINES

FRANCE

9 Specially Selected Vouvray Chenin Blanc 2020 £6.99

Richly coloured, honeysuckle and apple-blossom-scented classic Loire off-dry white; ideally balanced between ripe orchard-fruit lushness and tangy citrus acidity; 11.5% alcohol. Fine aperitif and a versatile partner for awkward menus of the likes of smoked fish, Asian dishes and salads. Thank you, Adrian and Catherine, for tipping this one.

GERMANY

9 Ockfener Bockstein Riesling Kabinett 2018 £6.49

Fab racy moselle (well, Saar tributary, strictly speaking) from the Classic Icons range. Available only online but a very welcome addition to the Aldi range – a sign, I hope, that this German enterprise will offer more of its native wines. Fine, apple-crisp and floral-spicy gently grapey riesling character; 11.5% alcohol.

SPARKLING WINES

FRANCE

10 Crémant de Jura 2019 £8.49

Latest in more than a decade of good vintages for this excellent traditional-method pure-chardonnay sparkler from the mountainous region of Jura east of Burgundy. Thrillingly fresh rush of pure ripe sweet-apple fruit in a persisting creamy mousse; 12% alcohol.

8 Veuve Monsigny No 111 Champagne Brut £12.99

This good-value, if occasionally inconsistent, house champagne is impressively cheap and generous with its apple-pie savour, carried along on a nice tide of bubbles; 12% alcohol.

Asda

If you're in economy mode – and who isn't right now – Asda should probably be your supermarket of choice. For wine, I mean. Aldi and Lidl hardly compare for bargains. Asda matches them for shelf prices, and then cuts further on individual 'rollback' deals. And Asda also offers regular across-the-board price promotions of 25 per cent off all wines. Sainsbury's, Tesco and others do the same, of course. But Aldi and Lidl never do.

Interesting, that. But there's a small drawback: Asda's range of wines is really not as enthralling as once it was. I have rather struggled to come up with the dozen recommended here, all of them wines I bought in my local big store. Asda did not ask me to their tasting this year, but I heard a whisper from one member of the press who had been honoured with an invitation that I hadn't missed much.

Well, boo. Let's suppose that this very large chain, lately taken over from US giant Walmart by enterprising petrol-station operators the Issa brothers, is in a period of retrenchment while they sort the financial side of the business out. In the present circumstances, I can imagine the sale of road fuels is a lot more rewarding than the retailing of wine.

RED WINES

CHILE

8 Cono Sur Pinot Noir 2020 £6.00

Good price for this stalwart varietal brand (also at Sainsbury's and elsewhere) with generous warmly developed cherry-berry fruit of satisfying heft; 13.5% alcohol.

9 Extra Special Carmenère 2020 £6.50

A return to form after a terrible 2019 vintage (okay it might have been a duff bottle) for this ripe and creamily oaked Colchagua bargain; cassis and black-cherry aromas, balanced bright fruit; 14% alcohol.

FRANCE

9 Grignan-les-Adhémar Cuvée Traditionelle 2020 £6.00

This is wishful thinking – that Asda will continue with this phenomenally good and good-value Rhône-area red, plumply delicious in this vintage (equal to the spiffy 2019) with red fruits including redcurrant, cherry, even cranberry, in a nicely weighted, juicy whole; 13.5% alcohol.

8 Extra Special Bordeaux Supérieur 2019 £7.00

Humble regional AP, revealingly ripe (2019 is a great Bordeaux year) and plummy with relishable flares of cinnamon and vanilla amid the textured blackcurrant savours; 13.5%. Picked this up, ignoring the dull label, for £6 on 'rollback'.

8 Extra Special Plan de Dieu Côtes du Rhône 2019 £8.00

Big wine from a rightly admired Rhône Villages zone fortuitously named 'God's Plain'. Full of warming, spicy hedgerow-ripe black fruit with plenty of woof (14% alcohol) and a brisk clean finish.

RED WINES

FRANCE

8 **Beaujolais-Villages Combe aux Jacques 2020 £11.00**
Hefty but joyously juicy vintage for this perennial and ubiquitous wine (also at Tesco among others) from grand Burgundy merchant Louis Jadot; 13.5% alcohol. It's not cheap, but look out for deals.

ITALY

8 **Extra Special Montepulciano d'Abruzzo 2020 £6.00**
Unsurprisingly up (though not that much, in the circs) on the £5.50 price for last year's very likeable 2019, this new vintage is particularly bright and juicy with proper bouncing regional style of raspberry-bramble fruit, pleasing heft (13.5% alcohol) and clean edge.

PORTUGAL

8 **Extra Special Douro 2020 £6.50**
Jolly cheap for a Douro red, made as it is from the prized fruit that goes into Port, this does have some of the heady aroma of the fortified wine and good dark, pruny-sweet black fruits; 13.5% alcohol.

PINK WINES

SPAIN

8 **Viña Albali Tempranillo Rosado 2020 £4.99**
Plenty of colour – magenta – to this mass-produced La Mancha pink. I chose it for a TV tasting largely because I thought the colour would come across well on camera. It did and the brisk, clean strawberry fruit was just fine; 11.5% alcohol. A fiver is as much as it is ever worth paying for rosé, I sometimes think.

WHITE WINES

FRANCE

8 **Extra Special Côtes de Gascogne Blanc 2021** **£6.00**
Crisp, party white with a crafty lick of richness in the middle fruit – very likeable at this keen price; 11.5% alcohol. Made by excellent regional co-operative Producteurs Plaimont.

GERMANY

9 **Dr L Riesling 2020** **£7.00**
This lovely moselle is still listed at Asda, and as long as it is, I believe there's hope for the supermarket's future as a wine retailer. It's an enticingly crisp green- and red-apple juicy riesling of startling freshness and intensity with a prickle of sherbet in the racy fruit; 8.5% alcohol.

ITALY

8 **Extra Special Fiano Terre Siciliane 2020** **£6.00**
The fiano was an early pioneer of the late-20th-century risorgimento among forgotten grape varieties believed to date from ancient Roman times, and made a welcome addition to the standard fare of generic Frascati and the like among Italian white wines. But fiano was soon superseded by cooler classical revivals falanghina, pecorino and so on. Shame. Do give this Asda number from Sicily a try: made by Settesoli, a leading island producer, it matches signature fiano blanched-almond and nectary plumpness with brisk citrus-nectarine twang and an appealing freshness; 12.5% alcohol.

SOUTH AFRICA

8 **Extra Special South African Sauvignon Blanc 2021** **£6.50**
I paid just £5.25 on promo for this and was impressed. Soft and ripe middle fruit in the Cape way with a crisp green grassy entry and lifting lemon tang at the finish; 13% alcohol.

The Co-operative

A Breath of fresh air. I was invited this year to taste new wines and new vintages from the Co-op for the first time since 2019, thanks to the Covid intermission, and it was great to be back.

I've had no difficulty finding more than 30 commendable wines for this entry, among them new additions including what I am calling my red wine of the year at under a tenner. It's Vergelegen Cabernet Merlot Fairtrade 2019 from South Africa. Vergelegen is one of the oldest and grandest estates in The Cape, producing sensational vintages at £50-plus, but the Co-op has persuaded the people there, who participate in the excellent Fairtrade scheme, to produce something for those of us on humbler budgets. The wine is a revelation. I cannot commend it enough – and the same goes for all those involved. The Co-op, please note, is the leading UK supporter of the Fairtrade scheme.

The Vergelegen wine is on shelf in 487 Co-op outlets (it says here) so you should be able to find it. If not, do remember the Co-op's find-a-stockist service online. You put in the wine you're after and your postcode and the names of the nearest stores ping up. Aren't computers wonderful?

RED WINES

ARGENTINA

8 **Co-op Irresistible Fairtrade Organic Malbec 2020** **£7.50**

Middling in weight but impressively intense in juicy black berry fruit, it's evidently oak-matured and accordingly sleek; 13% alcohol.

8 **Testimonio Cabernet Sauvignon Syrah Tannat 2020** **£10.00**

Darkly brooding Mendoza blend – note, no malbec in the mix – has silky blackcurrant savours with liquorice grippiness and a long luxury savour; 14% alcohol.

AUSTRALIA

8 **The Interlude Pinot Noir 2021** **£7.00**

This charming cherry-strawberry middleweight summer red is perkily ripe and comfortably short of sweet, staying poised to the edge of the flavour; 13.5% alcohol. Would respond well to fridge-time.

10 **Robert Oatley Semaphore Cabernet Sauvignon 2018** **£8.00**

Blood-red (in a nice way), concentrated, spicily savoury blackcurrant pure cabernet – endearingly wholesome and balanced with 14% alcohol. It's from a much-admired producer and feels very confidently made. Upfront in its flavours in the right Aussie tradition but really quite elegant. Good price.

8 **Bethany 6 Gen Old Vine Grenache 2021** **£10.00**

Big-hearted sweetly ripe but firmly trimmed and healthily spiced blackberry-juicy food red (cottage pie came to my mind) from the Barossa Valley; 14.5% alcohol.

RED WINES

FRANCE

9 Domaine Bisconte Roussillon 2018 £10.50

Red wines from Roussillon in the Midi often have an exotic distinctive fruits-of-the-forest spicy savour and this one fits. Deep maroon colour, peppery blackberry aroma, smooth and developed (though unoaked) round dark flavours with grippy tannin; 14.5% alcohol.

8 Château la Négly La Clape 2020 £12.00

Château la Négly is a renowned producer in the esteemed appellation of La Clape in the Languedoc. This unusually light-coloured and easy-weighted blend of regional varieties syrah, grenache and mourvedre is quite arrestingly good. Juicily ripe but firmly grippy, and showing warm garrigue character; 14.5% alcohol.

9 Château Haut-Bergey 2016 £20.00

This is delicious claret. It's from the well-rated appellation of Pessac-Leognan, just south of the city of Bordeaux, and made in the top-rated vintage of 2016. The colour is deep blood red, the nose has the trademark cedar/mint/cassis of serious bordeaux wine and the fruit is ripe and rich but poised, a lovely weight (13% alcohol) and the finish cleansing and lipsmacking. Perfectly mature, or you could give it longer. At twenty quid, is it worth it? To claret fans, definitely.

ITALY

9 Vanita Negroamaro 2020 £7.50

Splendidly labelled Puglian pasta red with cherries and chocolate on the nose and palate, and notions of prune and blackberry in the long fruit, niftily trimmed with nutskin-dry acidity; 13.5% alcohol. With apologies, I must use this space to mourn the delisting by the Co-op of this wine's white stablemate, the utterly brilliant Vanita Grillo. Co-op, how could you?

RED WINES

ITALY

10 Palladino Molise Biferno Riserva 2017 **£8.00**

Well, they're still listing this phenomenon from the obscure Italian east midlands, but it's now disappeared from all the stores near me and the price has gone up from last year's £7 – for the same vintage. To reiterate, you get a lush juicy scent from the montepulciano grapes in the mix and lots of ripe baked darker fruit flavours from aglianico, the other half of the blend. Joyously plumped from oak contact and relishing its maturity, this is a lovely vintage and long may it last; 13% alcohol.

8 Villa Antinori 2018 **£13.00**

Antinori is an aristocratic family wine business of old Florentine origin making fine Chiantis and other prestigious Tuscan specialties. Villa Antinori is their international export brand, a mix of regional sangiovese with Bordeaux varieties, and I have always admired it. This vintage is dark and cedary, plush with blackcurrant savour and slinky with 13.5% alcohol. Totally dependable and very likeable for what it is, even at the price.

8 Villa Boscorotondo Chianti Classico Riserva 2018 **£16.00**

The last vintage I tasted from this ornately named estate was the 2014, and it was so-so. This one is grand, grippingly firm with sour-cherry and smoky cassis flavour in the approved Chianti manner, luxuriantly velvety and luscious in the riserva (oak-aged) tradition; 14.5% alcohol. Authentic and authentically expensive, it's made by Tuscan legend John Matta of Castello Vicchiomaggio.

RED WINES

SOUTH AFRICA

8 Zalze Shiraz Grenache Viognier 2020 £7.85
Very ripe-tasting blackberry-fruit Fairtrade wine from dependable Zalze; a proper winter warmer in good balance; savoury richness from oak contact and 14.5% alcohol.

10 Vergelegen Cabernet Merlot Fairtrade 2019 £9.00
Vergelegen, est 1700, is a top Cape producer owned by mining giant Anglo American. Grand it might be, but Vergelegen also participates in the Fairtrade scheme, of which the Co-op is a major supporter. This wine, easily the best under-£10 red I've tasted all year, is not just ethically admirable, it's gorgeous. Clearly modelled on serious claret but with the extra heft and bloom imparted by Cape conditions to the slinky berry fruits and handsome grip; 14% alcohol. The price is a gift.

SPAIN

8 Jumilla Castillo de Zaln Monastrell 2020 £7.50
This is new to me at the Co-op; a muscular and wholesomely spicy food wine (meat, mainly) from organic Monastrell (Spain's name for the Mourvèdre of Mediterranean France). Darkly brambly and juicy with a proper sunny grip; 14% alcohol.

PINK WINES

FRANCE

8 Casanova Costa d'oru Rosé 2021 £7.50
Crisp Corsican wine with delicate geranium-pink hue, alluring apple-blossom and strawberry pong and convincingly lively and fresh corresponding fruit; 12.5% alcohol.

PINK WINES

FRANCE

8 Château Du Rouët Provence Rosé 2021 £8.50
The smart-looking printed bottle shows off the fine salmon colour to effect but what stood out for me was the welcome austerity of the fruit – tastes ripely pink, but not sweetly pink; 12.5% alcohol.

8 Mas De Origine Provence Rosé 2021 £14.00
I'm including this because Ben Cahill, Co-op buyer of French wines, tells me he particularly admires its colour, calling it 'rose quartz'. Given that colour is the principal appeal of rosé wine (in my book anyway) I do agree this fine, near-prickly-fresh dry wine scores very well in that respect; 13% alcohol.

8 Miraval Côtes de Provence Rosé 2021 £17.00
Cleverly contrived deluxe Riviera pink with elegant presentation, beguiling floral perfume and just the right balance of summer-red fruit and citrus tang; 13% alcohol. Famously owned by Brad Pitt, whose former partner (and spouse) Angelina Jolie, has since sold her half of the business to drinks giant Stoli. The wine hasn't suffered but the price is still eyewatering.

SPAIN

8 Cune Rioja Rosado 2020 £8.50
Softly ripe and strawberry-sweet but lifted by an artful citrus acidity, a nicely blush-coloured variation on the Rioja theme made largely from white viura grapes coloured with tempranillo; 12.5% alcohol.

WHITE WINES

AUSTRALIA

9 **The Interlude Coastal Chardonnay 2021** **£7.00**

Melon, peach, mango and nectarine all figure in the make-up of this lightly oaked Adelaide wine, somehow coalescing into an Aussie chardy significantly more crisply defined and honestly alluring than the usual brands. I really liked it and the price is right; 12.5% alcohol.

8 **Robert Oatley Signature Series Chardonnay 2020** **£11.50**

Deluxe, creamily-oaked, richly coloured, laa-dee-dah pure, mineral and plush special-occasion wine from famed vineyards of revered pioneer Bob Oatley; 12.5% alcohol.

CHILE

8 **Montes Reserva Chardonnay 2021** **£8.00**

This handsome Aconcagua brand has generous apple-pie-with-cream aromas and matching lush fruit, trimmed up nicely with citrus zest; exemplary Chilean chardy in the fuller style at a sensible price; 14% alcohol.

GERMANY

8 **Red Stone Gunderlich Riesling 2020** **£8.00**

New-style dry Rhine riesling with crisp apple and limey fruit, lively, fresh and distinctive; 11.5% alcohol.

8 **Von Kesselstatt Riesling Trocken 2020** **£12.00**

Prestige moselle, as dry as the trocken designation denotes – the front label helpfully translates, bearing the legend 'Riesling Dry' – and it's a nice, crisply racy and fresh aperitif with 11.5% alcohol. Seems a bit expensive, though.

WHITE WINES

ITALY

7 **Co-op Orvieto Classico 2021** **£5.75**

Easy-drinking, sherbetty dry white – a cheery party wine. Orvieto, centred on a delectable hilltown of Umbria, was once a fashionable name and had its own distinct charms. This is not a wine of that kind, but it has a friendly freshness; 12.5% alcohol.

NEW ZEALAND

9 **Grove Mill Sauvignon Blanc 2021** **£7.00**

Assertive nettly mouthfiller (it says in my note) from Marlborough's much-vaunted Wairau Valley. Long on grassy lushness and lifted by brisk citrussy twang; 13% alcohol. Class act at a fair price.

PORTUGAL

7 **Vale Dos Pombos Vinho Verde 2021** **£6.00**

Water-white, palpably spritzy and grapey, low-tog (9.5% alcohol) recognisable Vinho Verde; fresh and not too sweet. Cheap too.

SOUTH AFRICA

8 **Co-op Fairtrade Irresistible Sauvignon Blanc Reserva 2021** **£6.50**

Very full of generous green-pepper fruit but balanced and grassily fresh too, a likeable dry wine in the best Cape style to go with food – fish, fowl, salads and so on; 12.5% alcohol.

WHITE WINES

SOUTH AFRICA

9 Cape Point Sauvignon Semillon 2021 £7.00
Rather ritzy oaked blend matching crisp sauvignon (86%) with lush pineappley semillon (14%) to form a ripe, refreshing food wine (shellfish, barbecue, canapes) of some gravitas at a keen price; 12.5% alcohol. All this, and Cape Point is a Fairtrade producer into the bargain.

SPAIN

8 Masterchef Verdejo 2021 £7.75
Yes, it's somehow connected to the popular BBC cooking contest. No, not sure why. Decent Rueda dry wine with full colour, brisk orchard fruits and almondy creaminess in the background; 13.5% alcohol.

FORTIFIED WINES

SPAIN

9 Romate Sanchez Amontillado Sherry £6.00
I can't remember seeing a proper sherry in the Co-op before and hope very much this one catches on. It's pale in colour for an amontillado, quite dry with good pungency, preserved-fruits and sweet nuts on the nose and palate, gentle smokiness; 17% alcohol. Serve chilled, serve generously.

SPARKLING WINES

ENGLAND

10 Balfour 1503 Foxwood Cuvee £17.50

Coruscating*. There's no better word for it. This Kentish glory from the champagne grape varieties chardonnay and pinot noir glitters gold in the glass, eagerly effervescing with the tiny bubbles that denote the best kind of sparkling wine made by the only proper method (yes, the champagne one). Brisk orchard fruit, a saucy suggestion of yeast and crisp freshness, with 12% alcohol. World-class fizz at a patriotic price. * From Latin *coruscare* to sparkle; figuratively or, as in coruscating wit, metaphorically.

FRANCE

9 Les Pionniers Champagne Brut £19.00

Named for the Rochdale Pioneers who launched the Co-operative movement in 1844 and made by esteemed champagne house Piper Heidsieck (est 1834), this is a crackingly good, lemon-meringue-pie scented non-vintage champagne of very good character. A fine balance of ripe sweet-apple fruit and tangy citrus freshness, long and uplifting with creamily persisting mousse; 12% alcohol.

Lidl

Just as I was going to press with this edition, I received a kind invitation from Lidl to come and taste a selection from their latest Wine Tour, all French, which sadly will have disappeared from the stores by the time this book goes on sale. Ho hum. But I certainly appreciate the gesture. It's several years since I last attended a Lidl tasting.

All the best wines they sell are, of course, from the six Wine Tours run through the chain each year. As they say at Lidl – endlessly – when they're gone they're gone. The wines left behind are the core range – a pretty miserable collection that is remarkably unchanging over time, and never seems to show any signs of expansion or improvement.

And so to this year's very brief round-up. All I can promise is that now tastings have resumed I can at least meet up with my old friend and Master of Wine Richard Bampfield, who chooses the wines, and see what he has to say.

RED WINES

ITALY

8 Chianti Riserva 2016 **£5.99**

Simple sour-cherry and redcurrant wine benefitting from time in the bottle (the 2016 is still the officially listed vintage); healthy and brisk at the finish; 13% alcohol.

8 Corte Alle Mura Chianti Riserva 2018 **£5.99**

I thought decent Chianti at this kind of price was long extinct but Lidl have chanced on this decent raspberry-sour-cherry balanced and authentic riserva (cask-matured) Tuscan classic, much more likeable in this vintage than of memory; 13% alcohol.

8 Barolo 2014 **£13.99**

It's crept – or rather leapt – in price from £9.99 not so long ago but this very decent vintage is worth it: coppery-ruby colour, affecting scent of cherries, roses and farmyard (well, sort of), and long, silky fruit with trademark Barolo semi-suspended heft; 14% alcohol. This is the vintage officially listed by Lidl, but I have seen the 2010 on sale in at least one branch.

NEW ZEALAND

8 Marlborough Pinot Noir 2020 **£7.99**

Extravagantly priced for Lidl, an authentic wine with ripe cherry-raspberry fruit and encouraging notions of earthiness and gentle spice, even of oak contact; 12.5% alcohol.

WHITE WINES

FRANCE

8 Val de Loire Sauvignon Blanc 2020 £6.49

Straightforward IGP pure-sauvignon from the grape's natural home, the Loire Valley, typical in its green, grassy perfume, crisp gooseberry-hinting fruit and brisk limey finish; 12% alcohol.

8 Chablis 2021 £13.00

I am amazed that Lidl persist with this perennial at such a price – it must have a following. And so it should. From the outset until last year, when it cost a bargain £9.99, this has consistently been a truly typical Chablis from the green-gold colour to the gunflint-mineral style of the lush green fruit and finely tuned acidity; 12% alcohol.

GERMANY

8 Thornicher St Michael Riesling 2021 £4.99

This crisp, even prickly, ripe-apple moselle of softly grapey charm is a modest 10.5% alcohol and alluringly inexpensive. I cannot understand why a teutonic enterprise such as Lidl pays so little heed to the wines of its fatherland.

FORTIFIED WINES

PORTUGAL

8 Armilar 10 Years Old Tawny Port £11.99

It's back! Ruby-coloured but tawny-character, sweetly nutty, figgy and creamy wood-aged wine by da Silva, much missed for several years, should be on shelf at least over Christmas, and is a real treat; 20% alcohol. Gary, please note for flask filling.

SPARKLING WINES

FRANCE

8 Crémant de Loire Brut £8.49

Creamily foaming sparkler from chenin blanc grapes with alluring lemon-meringue-pie aroma and matching briskly refreshing fruit, crisply dry but with a suggestion of the chenin blanc honeysuckle savour. Quality fizz at a fair price; 12% alcohol.

Majestic

After the gloom of Lidl, a joy to taste the wines at Majestic for the first time since 2019. After extricating itself from the bizarre relationship with 'Naked Wines' and tottering on the brink of closure, the warehouse chain has staged a convincing comeback and a jolly good tasting too.

Please take careful note that the prices quoted in the following pages are for 'Mix Six' purposes. As a rule, these are 10 to 20 per cent lower than single-bottle prices, recalling the far-off days when Majestic operated a minimum-purchase policy of 12 bottles, any mix, subsequently reduced to six bottles then dispensed with altogether.

It's a big range at Majestic but you can still expect to find nearly all the wines in every store, which is more than you can say for most of the supermarkets, and everything is also available online.

Particular strengths are Italy and Spain and there's always a decent choice of Beaujolais, including the rarer *crus*. Majestic has forever prided itself on the depth of its champagne range, but its prices don't look too attractive just at the moment. Mix Six included.

My top picks this year include an outstanding Chilean syrah, an exceptionally good-value everyday claret and a pair of Romanian wines offering a timely reminder that not all is utterly tragic in the realms of the former Soviet bloc.

RED WINES

ARGENTINA

9 **Bodegas Fabre Alta Yari Gran Corte 2019** **£16.99**

A claret-inspired blend of two parts cabernet franc to one of malbec with a little cabernet sauvignon by Bordeaux-born Hervé Joyaux Fabre, who moved to Argentina 30 years ago. This lovely wine is dark and dense in the Mendoza manner but elegant in its black-fruit savours and cedary succulence in the French tradition; 14.5% alcohol. Artfully delicious and generously reduced from the single-bottle price of £24.99.

CHILE

10 **Mayu Titon Vineyard Syrah Gran Reserva 2017** **£9.99**

From the Elqui Valley, known equally for its observatories – the skies above are among the planet's clearest – as its unique vineyard conditions, this extraordinary near-black, sweetly roasted and spiced pure syrah as much resembles a classic, restrained northern Rhône red like St Joseph as it does the softer southern-hemisphere style. It's gorgeous, balanced and fascinating; 14.5% alcohol.

8 **Mayu Carmenère Appassimento 2018** **£9.99**

Made with a mix of normally ripened fruit with bunches left on the vine for seven weeks longer, this quirky concoction has an appropriately raisiny but wholesome aroma, darkly browning colour and caramelly fruit, all niftily balanced and grippy with savoury tannins; 14.5% alcohol. Experimental and fun.

RED WINES

FRANCE

8 Jean Chatelier Les Davaines Gamay 2021 £7.99
Gamay is the grape of Beaujolais and this Coteaux du Lyonnais (small AC neighbouring Beaujolais) is something akin, light in colour and heft but sincere in intention, a ripely juicy refresher to drink cool; 12% alcohol.

8 Naudin Père et Fils Pinot Noir 2020 £8.99
Made by an old Savigny-les-Beaune family firm this is a big-flavoured farm burgundy: bold colour, sweet cherry/raspberry nose, full corresponding fruit and wholesome grip; 13% alcohol.

10 Château Recougne 2018 £9.99
It's a humble generic right-bank Bordeaux Supérieur but this merlot-based claret speaks clearly of quality winemaking, succulently ripe and developed in its naturally silky flavours at a very fair price; 14.5% alcohol. Absolutely stands out from what is a very large claret crowd around this price level.

8 Definition Fleurie 2021 £10.99
I don't believe the producers of this wine, Eric Pardon and his son Jean-Marc, have anything to apologise for this year. The Beaujolais crus had a reduced harvest in 2021, but quality looks good, with this wine showing gravitas and juicy intensity of fruit; only just bottled when I tasted it, I think it will turn out well; 13% alcohol.

9 Château de Pizay Brouilly 2020 £11.99
Lush, concentrated classic Beaujolais from the always alluring cru of Brouilly has violet and cranberry suggestions on nose and fruit and proper juicy bounce all the way through to the crisp finish; 13% alcohol.

RED WINES

FRANCE

8 Henri Pion Bourgogne Rouge 2018 £16.99

This generic burgundy from the Côte d'Or, as distinct from the junior appellations of Chalonnais and Mâconnais whence come most generic burgundy, is all pinot noir, showing a fine jewel colour and really rather grand pinot fruit, slick with strawberry/raspberry ripeness, long and pleasingly plump; 13% alcohol.

8 Château Batailley Lions de Batailley 2015 £34.99

Château Batailley is a grand cru classé of the commune of Pauillac in Bordeaux's Médoc currently making fabulous claret at prices reasonable for its level – about £70 for this vintage of the grand vin. This 'second' wine at half the price is more than half as good (yes, I have tasted the sublime 2015) and I believe claret fanatics can invest with confidence. Lovely now, silky and sleek with grippy blackcurrant force and cedar notes and 13.5% alcohol it should develop for years.

ITALY

9 937 Polvanera Organic Primitivo 2021 £8.99

Puglian wine from a Marchesana estate founded only 20 years ago is a dramatic deep maroon colour, sweetly perfumed with violets and black cherries, opulent in its velvety fruit and nicely taut at the finish; seriously good rendering of the rightly popular primitivo theme; 14.5% alcohol.

8 Cecchi Governo All'uso Toscano 2020 £8.99

It's a Chianti reviving governo, an old technique of plumping up the wine by adding concentrated must late in the fermentation, making for a richer, darker style of wine; seems to succeed well here in this bold sour cherry contrivance; 13% alcohol.

RED WINES

ITALY

9 **Cantine Vitevis Ca'Vegar Valpolicella Superiore 2020** **£10.99**

Inky ruby colour has more intensity than I expect from Valpolicella, and the lush but nicely abrading fruit has more heft too, fine cherry-mocha-nutty notes, very bright and juicy, finishing very clean; 13% alcohol. Very good wine of its kind.

ROMANIA

10 **Incanta Pinot Noir 2020** **£6.49**

Pale, plump and perky juicy raspberry-cherry pure varietal co-produced by Majestic with resident winemakers Hartley Smithers and Nora Iriarte in Romania. Incanta in Romanian means 'delight' and this delectable pinot lives up to it; 12.5% alcohol. Definitely one of the bargains of the year.

SOUTH AFRICA

9 **Reyneke Vinehugger Organic Red 2020** **£10.99**

From syrah with a tiny bit of cabernet sauvignon, a huge ripe spicy-black winter warmer of a very sunny disposition somehow finely poised and ideally weighted; 14% alcohol. Thoroughly seductive Sunday roast treat.

8 **Gabb Family Vineyards Cabernet Sauvignon 2019** **£10.99**

Stellenbosch pure varietal from a WWF-awarded carbon-negative estate is grippingly good with muscular, oak-smoothed blackcurrant succulence lit by a fine leafy savour; 14% alcohol.

PINK WINES

FRANCE

8 **Abbotts & Delaunay Les Fruits Sauvage Grenache Rosé 2021** **£8.99**

Pale but interesting, fresh and crisp natural-tasting Languedoc dry wine – a change from the ubiquitous Provence style at a reasonably sensible price; 12.5% alcohol.

PINK WINES

GREECE

8 **Skouras Cuvée Prestige Rosé 2021** **£8.99**

Nicely made Peloponnese just-dry, generously pink-tasting food wine for holiday drinking; 13% alcohol.

ITALY

8 **Nero Oro Rosé 2021** **£8.99**

Attractive petal colour to this Sicilian gently-dry refresher from briefly macerated nerello mascalese grapes and properly pink-tasting soft-red-summer-fruit savours; 12.5% alcohol.

8 **Lugana Tommasi Le Fornaci Rosé 2021** **£11.99**

I'm a fan of the elegant dry whites of Lugana on the shores of Lake Garda, and here's a novelty: pink Lugana from turbiana, the grape that makes the white wines, mixed with rondinella, one of the black grapes constituent in local red Valpolicella. Result: delicate colour, redcurrant-raspberry notes in the scent and crisp, defined fruit, plenty of interest and refreshment, at a price; 12.5% alcohol.

ITALY

8 **11 Minutes Rosé 2021** **£15.99**

Couldn't resist this flesh-pink curio from Verona cantina Pasqua clearly aimed at the nerd market. The 11 minutes are those for which the new-pressed juice stays in contact with the crushed red skins of the constituent grapes to impart the delicate colour before being run off. Many pink wines are made simply by mixing red and white must. This very proper vino is delightfully blossom-fragrant, plump but fresh and definitely pink-tasting; 12.5% alcohol. The price is fair enough.

WHITE WINES

AUSTRALIA

9 Shaw & Smith M3 Chardonnay 2020 £29.99

Top-drawer chardy from vineyards (one called M3) established by legendary pioneers Martin Shaw and Michael Hill Smith that has to be one of Australia's best. The vines grow at altitude in the Adelaide Hills overlooking the ocean, and these conditions no doubt contribute to the rare character of the finished product. This vintage (the first was in 2000) is pale gold with emerald flashes, has thrilling peachy-grapefruit aromas and lush but mineral poised fruit; it's barrel fermented but the richness comes from the ripeness of the fruit rather than the vanilla-kiss of oak; 13.5% alcohol. Fabled wine at a modest price compared to the white burgundies it may or may not aspire to equal.

AUSTRIA

8 Schloss Massau Quittengang Grüner Veltliner 2018 £15.99

Richly coloured, exotic aromatic but balanced and very dry-finishing superior, mature food wine (a ceremonial carp comes quickly to mind) manifesting all the virtues of Austria's national white grape; 13% alcohol.

FRANCE

8 Duffour Père et Fils Vinum Côtes de Gascogne 2021 £6.99

The green grassy whiff off this sherbetty-twangy dry wine leads into an enjoyably nuanced combo of white-fruit savours, refreshing and stimulating; finishes crisp and clean; 11.5% alcohol.

WHITE WINES

FRANCE

8 **Abbotts & Delaunay Les Fruits Sauvages 2020** **£8.99**

Languedoc wine with Burgundian pretensions. Fine gold colour, sweet-apple and citrus perfume and lush peachy fruit with a heft of new-oak richness, nicely judged; 13.5% alcohol.

8 **Coup de Tête Beaujolais Blanc 2020** **£9.99**

White Beaujolais is all chardonnay, a sort of novelty wine, but has its own appeal, as in this plump apple-strudel dry wine with a lick of caramel and a lift of citrus acidity; nicely made and fun; 13% alcohol.

8 **Louis Violland Mercurey Blanc 2018** **£9.99**

Mercurey is an individual appellation of the Chalonnais, a satellite region of Burgundy, and a good source of affordable quality chardonnay in the regional manner. This barrel-fermented and aged wine is a fine introduction: richly coloured, sweet-apple and citrus perfume, plush limpid ripe fruit with mineral zest and 13.5% alcohol.

8 **Definition Chablis 2021** **£14.99**

Made for Majestic by scale Chablis producer Moreau, this is in the richer 'Côte d'Or' style but unoaked, plump but zingy with proper gunflint nose and lime-juice acidity; 12.5% alcohol.

8 **Parcel Series Sauternes 2018** **£14.99**

Ambrosial, honeyed – but ideally balanced – stickie presumably from a prestigious cru classé château as Majestic insists the origin is 'confidential'; 14% alcohol. The mix six price really is a bargain for this quality, and also in the context of the single-bottle price at £24.99.

WHITE WINES

GERMANY

10 Dr Hermann Ürziger Würzgarten Riesling Auslese 2006 — £16.99

In last year's edition I praised the 2005 vintage of this epic moselle to the skies. My expectations of the succeeding vintage were low, however, as 2006, a poorly-rated year, has none of the reputation of its perfect-conditions predecessor. Well, never mind that. The good Dr Hermann has triumphed yet again with this ravishing gold 'sweet' wine made rich by the occult late-harvest methods of the Mosel; it's at once honeyed and racy, apple-strudel unctuous and twangy with citrus. A great wine in the pomp of maturity with just 8.5% alcohol. Well done Majestic in offering this rare kind of wine: nobody else in the high street seems to bother.

ITALY

8 Domini Veneti Soave Classico 2021 — £8.99

Gold-green colour, grassy-lemon nose with a trace of blanched almond, zesty fresh white fruits and crispness all the way through – proper Soave; 12.5% alcohol.

8 Sirch Friulano Colli Orientali del Friuli 2021 — £9.99

The quirky friulano grape indigenous to Friuli in northeast Italy is a Venetian favourite for its broad intense flavours embracing peach and melon, marzipan and orange, all in a refreshing dry medium. This one fits the bill: basket of flavours, likeable weight and balance, long brisk finish; 13.5% alcohol.

8 Feudi di San Gregorio Greco di Tufo 2021 — £14.99

Made by Pierpaolo Sirch, also responsible for the nifty Friulano above. A fine and expensive dry wine from the Campania region, east of Naples. The greco grape is so called because it was probably imported by Greek settlers more than 2,500 years ago, and tufo is the soil formed from volcanic ash. The wine is uniquely mineral and aromatic in its nature, much prized for its exciting pear-lemon-nutty savours and low-acid lushness. This is just so, lively but complex, a versatile menu matcher; 13% alcohol.

WHITE WINES

NEW ZEALAND

9 Villa Maria Seaspray Sauvignon Blanc 2021 £13.99

Wildly aromatic wine from famed Kiwi producer's coastal vineyards at Awatere lives fully up to its maritime name with zingy beach-grass aromas, long nettly green fruits, lime zest and crisp edge; 14% alcohol. New Zealand sauvignon as a genus needs to keep expanding its horizons and this one succeeds.

PORTUGAL

8 Casal de Ventozela Vinho Verde 2021 £7.99

Leesy VV with less spritz and more crunchy white fruit and lemon zest than usual brands, and yet it is really quite dry (most export VVs are sweetened); 12% alcohol.

ROMANIA

9 Incanta Chardonnay 2021 £6.99

This really delivers: made with a tiny addition of local feteasca grapes, a nuanced dry wine with a lick of sweet-apple-pie lushness and a stimulating minerality; 13% alcohol.

SPAIN

9 Martin Codax Albariño 2020 £8.99

The co-operative of Martin Codax, formed in 1986, made the name of the DO Rias Baixas in Atlantic Galicia with the distinctive crisp-fruit flavours of the albariño grape, grown on high trellises for maximum exposure to sunlight and sea breezes. A joy to taste this seminal wine, always championed by Majestic, again after many years and the proliferation of strong competitors. It still leads the way: long and lush with limey zest and crunchy white fruits; 12.5% alcohol.

SPARKLING WINES

ENGLAND

9 Louis Pommery Brut England £27.99

To all intents and purposes, this is champagne. It's made in Kent by Vranken Pommery, heir to the grande marque champagne house Pommery & Greno, est 1860, which bought land in Kent a few years back, planted the usual champagne grapes and now is the first of the maisons (others will follow) to market their own English brand, coyly describing it as made by 'the traditional method'. Well, I love it. It looks and tastes like champagne, and jolly good champagne with elegant poise and a fine rush of foaming fruit-brioche-refreshing savours; 12.5% alcohol. But it's British, and cheaper than its begetter's domestic brands. The shape of things to come?

SPAIN

9 The Guv'nor Sparkling NV £8.99

Almost fiercely fizzy cava blend of chardonnay with viura has lashings of crisp orchard fruit and a sneaky creaminess (some oaked wine in the mix) alongside the refreshing tangy acidity; 12% alcohol. An artful contrivance at a good price.

Marks & Spencer

It was a marvel to be at the Marks & Spencer tasting – for the first time since 2019. How things have moved on. Two new ranges, Classics and 'Found' have kicked off since last time round and I had only tried a very few of them. Here, you'll find numerous wines from both these lines among the 57 featured.

Countless old M&S favourites have been dropped, presumably to make way for all these additions, and given how good so many of the new wines are, I'm not getting sentimental about it.

The 'Found' range is particularly inspired. All are from off-beat locations and/or obscure grape varieties and I like the arty black-and-white period photographs that illustrate the labels. On the whole, they refer only very obliquely to the places the wines have been found, and that's fine with me.

I am particularly impressed with the value for money M&S are giving. Of the 50-odd still wines I've liked so much only one costs above a tenner, and there is plenty of choice between £6 and £8 – to me, a crucial level for affordable quality. M&S do offer regular promotions, both in the stores and online. Note, though that sales online are still exclusively six-bottle cases at a time. And, of course, many M&S wines are now offered by Ocado.

A special mention for English sparkling wine Bramble Hill at £15.00. It's the first home-grown fizz of any manifest quality made by the 'tank' or 'Charmat' method that I have tasted. And I loved it. The sparkling-wine lady at M&S was at pains to assure me it was not made by the 'champagne' method because I was sceptical, given how convincingly busy and persistent the bubbles were. But yes, Bramble Hill is produced by the same bulk method as prosecco. It's a million times better, and it's ours!

RED WINES

ARGENTINA

8 Rastras Malbec 2021 £7.50
Easy-drinking, likeably new-leather-scented and generously upholstered young Mendoza barbecue wine of typical charm; 13% alcohol.

8 Facón Grabado Malbec 2020 £10.00
Opaque maroon colour to this Mendoza toasty-oaked pure malbec, a muscular rendering of the darkly savoury theme with notes of coffee and bitter chocolate amid the black, black fruit. 14% alcohol.

AUSTRALIA

8 Dog on the Tuckerbox 'Jammy' Shiraz 2021 £7.00
Terrible presentation but enjoyable, spicy barbecue wine. Not in the least 'jammy' as in the common fault of cloying sweetness, but savoury, balanced and healthy; 13.5% alcohol.

8 d'Arenberg The Shepherd's Clock GSM 2019 £10.00
Grenache, shiraz and mourvèdre blend by McLaren Vale legend Chester Osborne with intensity of colour, ripeness and spice all in gently gripping harmony; 14.5% alcohol. New to M&S this year and well worth a try.

AUSTRIA

8 Found Zweigelt 2021 £8.50
New addition to the impressive 'Found' range from Austria's native black grape the zweigelt, named after its 1922 creator Dr Zweigelt. Pale in the manner of pinot noir with sweet black-cherry perfume and deliciously juicy raspberry fruit, healthily dry and balanced; 13% alcohol. I would serve this fridge cool.

RED WINES

CHILE

8 **Ya'Po Merlot 2021** £6.00

Chile has its own way with merlot: this bargain's sweet but not at all confected, artfully taut in its black-cherry/bramble juiciness, wholesome and 13% alcohol.

8 **Tierra Y Hombre Pinot Noir 2021** £7.50

Casablanca perennial on good form: sweetly ripe, cherry-raspberry, plumply oaked pure-fruit classic Chilean pinot at a sensible price; 13.5% alcohol.

FRANCE

8 **Cahors Malbec 2020** £8.00

This generic wine is impressively dark maroon in colour with spicy blackberry pong and sinewy-savoury matching fruit with a firm grip on the tastebuds; 13.5% alcohol.

8 **Classics Claret 2020** £8.00

Nice ripe merlot-based wine by reliable Sichel – lightish in ruby colour but satisfying in intensity (13.5% alcohol) with a hint of mint and leaf to the cassis and a decent grip.

GERMANY

9 **Palataia Pinot Noir 2020** £9.00

This is a kind of Rhine burgundy, pure pinot noir from the vineyard of M&S's very own Winzer Gerd Stepp, formerly a staffer, now an estate owner in the Pfalz. It's lush with cherry-raspberry fruit, earthy and mineral with plenty of plumpness (and 13.5% alcohol), a lovely, satisfying wine of its own kind.

RED WINES

GREECE

10 Found Xinomavro Mandilaria 2020 £9.50

A triumphant follow-up to last year's 2019 vintage, this has lovely glowing ruby hue, luscious cassis fruits and remarkable weight and balance. It's from a famed Macedonian winemaker who blends xinomavro grapes grown in Greece's best-rated vineyard region Naoussa with mandilaria from the Aegean's ultra-trendy resort island Santorini, blown apart by a vast volcanic explosion 3,500 years ago and now making fabled wines in the residual landscape. This is wine with a story, and that's always the best kind of wine; 13.5% alcohol.

ISRAEL

9 Racanati Petite Sirah 2020 £10.00

From vineyards in Galilee and the Judean Plain, this is darkly, spicily sleek and juicy, ideally weighted (13.5% alcohol) and trimly finished. Who would guess its biblical origins?

ITALY

9 Found Nerello Cappuccio 2020 £7.00

From Sicily's near-hyperactive co-operative Settesoli, a deeply coloured, bitter-chocolate-hearted black-fruit pasta red of intense savour from one of the island's rarer native grapes, distinctive, complex, satisfying and good value; 13.5% alcohol.

8 Castello Perduto Valpolicella 2020 £7.00

This fine example of a long-renowned and happily enduring Lake Garda wine has light structure but good intensity, textbook sour-cherry fruit and a clean nutskin finish. Perfect complement to sticky pasta, risotto and the like, and a fine red aperitif out of the fridge; 12.5% alcohol.

RED WINES

ITALY

8 **Burchino Governo all'Uso Toscana 2018** £9.00

Governo is an old Chianti trick of adding concentrated must to the fermented wine to cause a secondary ferment, enlivening the finished product. The practice died out decades ago but now it's back, making fun, rich, toasty passito-like wines such as this one. I liked its dense blackberry-cherry fruit, chocolate heart and nicely abrading finish; 14% alcohol. New to M&S this year.

9 **La Prendina Estate Bardolino 2020** £10.00

Bardolino can be a bit weedy, but not this one. Bright jewel-like colour, big whiff of cherry and seductive cherry-almondy-redcurrant typical fruit finishing snappy-crisp but lingering in its savour; 13% alcohol. Super, distinctive red wine to match saucy fishy dishes as well as meatier fare.

8 **Pontenari Toscana Rosso 2020** £12.00

It's a kind of 'supertuscan' mix of two-thirds sangiovese, the Chianti grape, and one-third cabernet and merlot, the Bordeaux varieties. Result: intense beetroot colour, dense cassis and sour-cherry fruit with firm tannin. a bit of oak contact and, I'd guess, potential longevity; 14% alcohol.

PORTUGAL

8 **Found Alicante Bouschet 2021** £9.00

Alicante is a grape that flourishes in Portugal's Alentejo region and unconnected to the resort in Spain. This new find at M&S has a fine sheeny maroon colour, trademark Portuguese black-fruit savours referencing clove, cinnamon and mint, easy weight and gently grippy acidity; 14% alcohol.

RED WINES

SOUTH AFRICA

8 **Bosman VIII Generation Merlot 2021** £9.00

Deluxe new-oak-matured pure merlot, sleek with black-cherry ripeness balanced by friendly tannins. Good intensity and weight, a fine tribute to the sometimes-overlooked delights of Bordeaux's least-fashionable grape variety; 14% alcohol.

SPAIN

8 **Found Mazuelo 2019** £9.00

Lightish vegetal picnic wine from Mazuelo grapes grown in the eastern Rioja, packed with dark, brambly fruits, unoaked and quite unlike Rioja but deliciously lively and satisfying; 14.5% alcohol.

8 **Guia Real Rioja 2020** £9.00

Curiously named Rioja unconnected to M&S's continuingly excellent El Duque range; unoaked pure tempranillo with corresponding blackcurrant charm, eager and juicy with a good grip; 13% alcohol.

9 **El Duque de Miralta Rioja Crianza 2018** £10.00

Lovely maturing oaked pure tempranillo from M&S's excellent El Duque range made by distinguished El Coto bodega. Sweetly perfumed – roses and cream I've written here – with minty, slick cassis fruits, palpably natural-tasting and poised; 13.5% alcohol.

PINK WINES

FRANCE

9 Fleur de Lise Saint Mont Rosé 2021 £8.00

New wine to M&S by redoubtable Producteurs Plaimont in Gascony with discreet pale-copper colour, perfume of strawberry and other soft summer red fruits and a bright, brisk juiciness of style finishing very crisp; 12% alcohol. Exceptional, and good value.

8 Classic Côtes de Provence Rosé 2021 £9.50

Of the numerous M&S Provence pinks tasted on the day, I picked out this one as best and most sensibly priced (some were £15). Alpine strawberries is the core theme of the aroma and fruit, perky-fresh and finishing firmly dry; 13% alcohol.

GREECE

8 Myrtia Moschofilero Assyrtiko Rosé 2021 £10.00

Classy, holiday pink from the Peloponnese glows pale copper and balances crisp red fruit with limey twang, good assertive food matcher – anything under the sun; 12.5% alcohol.

PORTUGAL

8 Found Vinho Verde Rosé 2021 £7.50

Delicate petal pink colour and signature VV prickle in this (relatively) dry confection largely from touriga nacional (port) grapes make for a brisk, pleasingly fruity and pink-tasting refresher; 11% alcohol.

WHITE WINES

ARGENTINA

8 **Sabroso Pinot Grigio 2021** £6.00

I'm always prepared to try PG from outside its unnatural home of northeast Italy and this Mendoza effort certainly pips most of the grisly Veneto stuff, especially at such a keen price. Plenty of pleasing orchard fruit with notions of smoke and vegetal interest; 12.5% alcohol.

AUSTRALIA

8 **Burra Brook Sauvignon Blanc 2021** £7.00

This old favourite is a superior party dry white with 10% other varieties (including chardonnay) besides the sauvignon, and an agreeable medley of fresh green-fruit savours; 10.5% alcohol.

8 **d'Arenberg The Shepherd's Clock Chardonnay 2020** £10.00

New this year at M&S from a rightly famed McLaren Vale winery, this has gold colour, lush just-buttery sweet-apple fruit nicely spiced with cinnamon (?) and citrus and controlled oak enrichment; 13.5% alcohol.

AUSTRIA

9 **Classics Grüner Veltliner 2020** £8.50

From Austria's signature white grape, this stands out for its pairing of slaty minerality with slurpy exotic white fruits – such a fascinating, balanced aromatic dry wine and a very versatile meal matcher; 12% alcohol.

CHILE

8 **Ya'Po Sauvignon Blanc 2021** £6.00

New to M&S, a perky, pure party sauvignon with endearing goosberry-grassy green lushness and trademark Chilean sunny ripeness; 12.5% alcohol.

WHITE WINES

CHILE

8 **Classics Chilean Sauvignon Blanc 2021** **£8.00**
Casablanca wine shining with that generosity of ripeness that Chile has made a signature of its friendly sauvignons: full of colour, sweet-grass aromas and stimulating lively green fruits; 13.5% alcohol.

8 **Viña Moala Casa Clos Colchagua Chardonnay 2021** **£9.00**
My tasting note says 'a proper whack of agricultural fruit' by which I think I mean you get a big mouthful of natural and ripe chardonnay flavour; I liked it instinctively – lots of apple-strudel ripeness but nicely tight at the edge. A proper food wine for shellfish, chicken etc; 13.5% alcohol.

FRANCE

8 **Côtes du Rhône Blanc Les Remparts 2021** **£8.00**
Rich in colour and heft with complex basket-of-fruit ripeness balanced by keen citrus acidity, an exotic but definitely dry white for food matching; 13% alcohol.

8 **Bordeaux Sauvignon Blanc 2021** **£9.00**
A faultless pure-sauvignon by rated Sichel company, spare but lush, grassy and classy, 12% alcohol. Bordeaux's spin on the world's favourite white grape is unique: do give this fine example a try.

8 **Classics Alsace Gewürztraminer 2020** **£10.00**
Richly coloured, lychee and rose-petal-scented, aromatic, not-too-sweet wine is perhaps unusually ripe (14% alcohol) but in good balance and capable of matching all sorts of exotic menus. Definitely a step up from most supermarket Gewürz.

WHITE WINES

FRANCE

8 **Mâcon Villages 2020** £10.00

Immediately likeable, leesy-sherbetty pure-chardonnay in the distinctively lemony-herby Mâconnais manner, not oaked but plumply ripe and healthy; 12.5% alcohol.

GERMANY

9 **Classics German Riesling 2020** £9.50

Full but racy with green-apple crispness and grapily ripe, a luscious Rheinpfalz wine from M&S's very own riesling genius Gerd Stepp. Made in the modern style, it's 12% alcohol and a fine food wine – poultry comes to mind, as well as seafood, Asian dishes and charcuterie.

10 **Found Weißburgunder 2021** £9.50

Simply perfect pinot blanc from the Rheinpfalz-region winery of former M&S staffer and now star winemaker Gerd Stepp. Beautiful gold colour, peary-appley-fresh with a suggestion of blanched almond in aroma and fruit, racy and fresh, referencing the Alsace style – yes, difficult to explain, but gorgeous; 12.5% alcohol. Top buy new to M&S this year, and a revelation.

HUNGARY

8 **Found Furmint 2021** £8.00

Impactful, ripely grapey and refreshing dry wine from the variety better known for making Hungary's super-sweet Tokay. This one has exotic notions of smokiness over fruits evoking quince, apricot and citrus – distinctive and delicious; 12% alcohol.

ITALY

8 **Vermentino Sicilia 2021** £6.50

From redoubtable Sicily co-op Cantine Settesoli, a likeably austere refresher ranging in reference from greengage to nectarine with lifted citrus and proper Italian identity; 12.5% alcohol.

WHITE WINES

ITALY

10 Found Ribolla Gialla 2021 £7.50

What's this? 'Ribolla gialla is an ancient gem of a variety found in the north east of Italy', says M&S, 'where the Bora wind from the Dolomites helps retain freshness in this bright yellow "gialla" coloured grape'. Got the flavour? I loved it: creamily eggy but pure mineral orchard-fruit, lemon-lifted emphatically Italian dry white of irresistible charm; 12.5% alcohol. Adaptable pasta/poultry/fish/salady wine.

8 Terre di Chieti Pecorino 2021 £8.00

Wordy label makes a change from the usual sheep theme on this wholesome Abruzzo dry white from Pecorino grapes (nonsensically associated with a ewe's milk cheese of the same name) with peachy, green-herb and citrus notes and elegantly poised freshness; 12% alcohol.

8 Bella Verità Organic Falanghina 2021 £9.00

Falanghina, believed to have been the favourite white grape of boozy Ancient Rome under the name Falernian, is currently cool and this one lives up to the hype: tangy-fresh with crisp apple and pear juiciness and a pronounced citrus lift, this Puglian rendition has timeless charm; 12.5% alcohol.

PORTUGAL

8 Classics Vinho Verde 2021 £8.00

Palpable spritz, lots of lemon-gold colour and zippy characteristic white nettly fruit; it's dry by usual VV standards but full of interest and just 10% alcohol.

WHITE WINES

ROMANIA

10 **Found Feteasca Regala 2021** £7.00

It's from a historic Transylvanian winery formerly maladministered by Marxist masters but in these post-Soviet times managed by an Englishman, Philip Cox, and his Romanian wife Elvira. Fine, exotic, just-dry wine poised between evocations of peachy plumpness and spiced, crisp apple juiciness; 11.5% alcohol. Stands out as both an aperitif and adaptable food partner.

SOUTH AFRICA

8 **This is Vibrant & Zesty Sauvignon Blanc 2021** £5.00

Very decent Cape crisp sauvignon with green-pepper freshness and satisfying heft; 12.5% alcohol. Amazingly cheap.

8 **Found White Grenache 2021** £8.00

Impressive new vintage to follow up the launch in 2020 of this well-found Cape wine in what I call the Alsace style; plenty of plump white melon-peach aroma and fruit, an interesting vegetal heft and fine grapefruit twang to finish; 14% alcohol.

9 **22 Families Old Bush Vine Chenin Blanc 2021** £9.00

Delicately poised between honeysuckle aromas and racy twang, a very reassuring Swartland dry wine making the most of the chenin blanc's brilliance of balance; 12.5% alcohol. Cape chenin is one of the emerging wonders of the wine world.

WHITE WINES

SOUTH AFRICA

8 **Journey's End Honeycomb Chardonnay 2020** **£9.00**

This is very much an oaked chardonnay, with most of the blend fermented in casks and all of it matured for six months in French barriques. It's generously creamy in its ripeness (13.5% alcohol) but crisply defined in lifted sweet-apple fruit; you know you've got a grown-up wine.

SPAIN

8 **Monte Lagares Rioja Blanco 2020** **£8.00**

In the modern unoaked almost-steely dry style of white Rioja, a good effort if that's your preference; 12.5% alcohol.

FORTIFIED WINES

SPAIN

8 **M&S Dry Fino Sherry** **£9.00**

By Bodegas Williams & Humbert of Dry Sack fame, an unexpectedly coloured 'pale' fino with assertive yeasty floral nose and full pungent keen fruit; by no means bone-dry but finishes refreshingly crisp with citrus tang; 15% alcohol. Characterful, likeable and decent value.

SPARKLING WINES

ENGLAND

10 Bramble Hill English Sparkling **£15.00**

Breakthrough wine: it's made from English-grown champagne grapes but not by the champagne method of secondary fermentation in bottle. Instead, it's made in a massive tank, like prosecco. But this isn't like prosecco – it's 'brut', very dry in style but abounding with crisp orchard fruits and notes both of yeast and of citrus – much like champagne; 12% alcohol. And it's properly sparkling, nothing like prosecco's dying fizzle. I loved it and had not guessed its tank (or 'Charmat') provenance until told so by M&S's sparkling wine buyer, who explained that the maker of this wine, Jerome Barret, is a dab hand at giving tank sparklers a particularly persistent mousse. He's a genius. I hope this wine is a pioneer of a whole new class of English sparklers at sensible prices.

FRANCE

9 Found Blanquette de Limoux **£10.00**

Fine gold colour, busy-busy froth and flush with crisp orchard fruits enriched with yeasty bakery aromas and flavours, this is an extraordinarily good sparkling wine; 12% alcohol. Made largely from Mauzac grapes (once called Blanquette) of the Midi by the traditional method (once called the champagne method), it is a delight.

8 Champagne Delacourt Brut **£22.00**

Pleasingly mellow house champagne has crisp red-apple fruit savours and biscuity glow amid the busy tiny-bubble frothiness; 12.5% alcohol. This brand replaced M&S's forever champagne, Oudinot (much missed by me) five years ago at a launch price of £30. At the present price it is much more rational value.

SPARKLING WINES

FRANCE

9 **Champagne Delacourt Medium Dry** **£22.00**

This wine has the same cépage or grape-mix as its brut version above, but an added sugar measure of 36 grammes per litre instead of the brut's 8 g/l. The difference? This medium-dry style has a yielding softness – not sweetness – to the appley/bready savours and less of the greenness of acidity of the brut style; 12.5% alcohol. I think it's a marvel, and perfect for keen celebrants who can find champagne 'sharp'.

Morrisons

It was only in June 2022 that the American private equity outfit Jackal Vulture & Eviscerator, or whatever it's called, finally got the nod from the UK's competition regulator to swallow up Morrisons. So, it's a bit early to estimate what effect the £7 billion takeover will have on the operations of this fine old Yorkshire-born family enterprise.

And it's a bit awkward for me to report on the current state of the wine offering, as Morrisons didn't ask me to their 2022 press tasting. Cheers, Morrisons. But I have been undaunted. For the third year in a row, I've been out buying the wines at my nearest branches, taking full advantage of the regular promotional offers, in particular the perpetual deals on 'The Best' own-label range: buy any three bottles and save 25 per cent. Very useful savings.

Most of the wines on the following pages are consequently from this range, and jolly good they are. I have awarded maximum points to the Chablis AC and Soave and have picked out several bargains I got for not much more than £5 and really liked. Perhaps I had not really taken it in before that Morrisons is a bit of winner when it comes to budget wine-shopping – something an awful lot of us are going to have to get used to.

I hope it lasts. The bargain emphasis at Morrisons, I mean. Not the worldwide economic meltdown. Maybe Morrisons' proud new owners won't simply delete anything from the shelves that doesn't turn a sufficiently mighty dollar. Along with the retailer's 100,000-plus workforce and countless loyal suppliers, I guess we'll just have to wait and see.

RED WINES

ARGENTINA

8 **The Best Gran Montaña Malbec Reserve 2020** **£10.00**

I reviewed the 2016 vintage of this Uco Valley wine in the 2019 edition when it was priced at £12.00 and raved about it. This one, if memory serves, is less immediately appealing but I recognised the blackberry-blueberry juiciness amid the leathery grip of the ripe malbec and guess it might evolve in the bottle; 14% alcohol. I paid £7.50 on promo – good value.

FRANCE

9 **The Best Côtes du Rhône Villages 2020** **£7.00**

Glowing opaque beetroot colour and a nice pointy-spicy nose on this inky, concentrated, velvety but vigorous and agreeably peppery typical CdR, reportedly from grapes grown entirely in the well-designated Villages zone of Seguret; 14.5% alcohol. Good value.

8 **Monts & Vaux Malbec 2021** **£7.25**

Plain-wrapper Midi red with a nice twist of garrigue savour amid the juicy black malbec fruit; easy to like especially at the £5.25 I paid on promo; 12% alcohol.

9 **La Vieille Ferme Rouge 2020** **£8.00**

Another ace vintage – the 50th since since the brand's original launch – for this universal perennial by the Perrin dynasty of Châteauneuf du Pape's reverentially admired Château Beaucastel. This syrah-grenache blend from the nearly-neighbouring Luberon district is an artful contrivance of glowing ruby colour, cherry-pomegranate perfume and sleek black and red berry fruits; 13.5% alcohol. All this, and there's chickens on the label too. Always on discount somewhere – shop around.

RED WINES

FRANCE

8 The Best Fleurie 2020 £9.50

Now that Morrisons has dumped the phenomenally good Raoul Clerget Beaujolais AC that regularly top scored in this book at the very welcome price of a fiver, this will have to do as the next best thing. From the admired Beaujolais cru of Fleurie, it's nearly twice the price and not much better as an everyday juicy red refresher to drink cool; 13.5% alcohol. It does have the cheery purple cherry-raspberry bounce of the regional style, so that's all good then. On promo I paid a bit over £7.50, which is closer to what it's worth.

8 Heritages Côtes du Rhône 2021 £10.00

Earlybird red wine from the tricky 2021 vintage indicates that while it was a small harvest in the Rhône – down as much as a third on average – quality is looking just fine. This vigorously ripe blackberry-peppery new wine is intense but balanced and wholesome; 13.5% alcohol. Not cheap, mind.

ITALY

8 The Best Negroamaro 2021 £7.50

The noisy retro label doesn't flatter this dark, spicy and generous barbecue wine from reputable co-operative Cantina San Marzano (famed for spiffy pub favourite Il Pumo negroamaro) in Puglia, oak-plumped and tasting vigorously bright in its youth (note 2021 vintage); repays airing; 13.5% alcohol. I paid £5.63 on promo.

RED WINES

ITALY

7 The Best Valpolicella Ripasso 2018 £9.75

It's a matter of expectation. I bought this in a promo for about £8, partly driven on by the twin stickers appended to the gaudy label trumpetting 92 points from the 2021 IWC and 90 from Decanter. The wine looks good on pour: limpid deep ruby, and smells right – keen, heady sour-cherry Verona scents – but in the mouth it felt lean, even a little harsh. Good maybe in a defined fruit way, but lacking empathy; 13.5% alcohol. Look, it's just something to ponder, okay?

9 The Best Toscana 2019 £10.00

This perennial Morrisons-team-made favourite is distinctly Chianti-like in this new vintage, silky savoury and elegantly pitched in the manner of the region's best. A real hit. It's from sangiovese blended with cabernet sauvignon and merlot; 13% alcohol. I paid £7.50 on promo.

WHITE WINES

AUSTRALIA

8 The Best Western Australia Chardonnay 2020 £8.25

Made by the Ferngrove winery from the grapes of two top WA zones, Frankland and Margaret River, this is a wholesomely ripe chardy with minerality and citrus tautness nicely counterpointing the long, creamy apple-crumble fruit; there's some oaked wine in the blend and it works well; 13.5% alcohol.

WHITE WINES

AUSTRIA

9 The Best Grüner Veltliner 2020 £8.50

Remarkable gently pungent and stimulatingly refreshing dry wine from a seriously good producer, Markus Huber, in the Danube Valley of Austria's premier Niederösterreich region. The native grüner veltliner grape has a unique abrading style well worth getting to know; 12.5% alcohol.

FRANCE

8 Pomerols Picpoul de Pinet 2020 £8.50

Now well-established among fashionable Mediterranean seafood matchers, this is a dependable picpoul, crisp and bright with a discreet salinity and plenty of crunchy orchard fruit; 13% alcohol.

10 The Best Chablis 2020 £15.00

Fine new vintage of this dependable perennial with familiar greeny-gold colour, struck-match whiff and pebbly-fresh but lush white fruit – Chablis puts a genuinely unique spin on the chardonnay theme – and well-judged citrus twang; 12.5% alcohol. Price is up on last year's £13 but I paid just above £11 in a 25%-off-any-three-Best offer – now a very frequent Morrrisons promo – and that warrants maximum points.

ITALY

10 Morrisons Soave 2021 £4.85

Unbelievably cheap and the genuine article, attractively coloured, apple perfume, crisp matching fruit, blanched almond and lemon lift, simply delicious; 11% alcohol. The price is up on last year's barely believable £4.35, but this remains an extraordinary bargain.

WHITE WINES

ITALY

9 The Best Soave Classico 2020 **£7.75**

I believe this really is the best Soave Classico to be found at anywhere near this amazingly keen price. You get the right green-gold colour, tangy apple-sauce whiff and citrus lift in the crisp fruit with the signature trace of blanched-almond creaminess; 12% alcohol. Great stuff and occasionally on promo around six quid.

8 The Best Organic Verdicchio dei Castelli di Jesi 2020 **£7.00**

Lively but intriguingly nuanced dry food wine (Morrisons suggest spaghetti carbonara) from renowned DOC of Ancona in the Marches. Prickly-fresh and figgy-ripe; 12.5% alcohol. I paid just £5.25 on promo. The ancient city of Jesi grew up around a series of connected castles (castelli) built from the 4th century BC. The familiar amphora-shaped bottle evokes ancient times but dates back only to the 1950s, when the concept was first adopted in a regional marketing campaign.

8 The Best Falanghina 2020 **£7.25**

Well-coloured rancio dry wine from fashionable grape variety of the Campania (the region of Naples), plumply ripe with a grapefruit backnote and plenty of interest for food matching, especially healthy oily fish dishes; 12.5% alcohol. I paid £5.44 on promo.

SOUTH AFRICA

8 The Best Chenin Blanc 2021 **£7.50**

Another spiffy vintage for this model Swartland wine, delicately poised between honeyed ripeness and tangy citrus all through its aromas and flavours; 12.5% alcohol.

WHITE WINES

SOUTH AFRICA

8 **Klein Street Chardonnay 2021** **£7.50**

Pleased to see a new vintage of this good-value brand from a producer in the Cape Town region. A vivid and crisp chardonnay with reassuring plushness and notes of stone fruit en route to the correct citrus edge; 12.5% alcohol.

8 **The Best Grenache Blanc 2021** **£8.00**

From the same Swartland producer as the chenin blanc above, a fine apple'n'pear dry wine with intriguing traces of spice and nectarine; 12.5% alcohol. Grenache blanc from the Cape is always worth a try.

SPAIN

8 **The Best Marqués de los Rios Rioja Blanco Reserva 2018** **£13.00**

Lighter in colour and weight than preceding vintages, this is nevertheless still a revelation of times past, an oxidative creamy pineappley dry wine of real charm; 12.5% alcohol. I paid £9.75 in a 25%-off-any-3 Best promo.

FORTIFIED WINES

PORTUGAL

9 **Morrisons 10-Year-Old Tawny Port** **£12.00**

Still ruby in colour but showing encouraging signs of taking on the amber aspect known as 'tawny' in the Port trade, this silky cask-aged wine by Symingtons is quite delicious – the fieriness of the spirit in the blend mellowing nicely into the nutty-figgy-orange-peel fruit; 20% alcohol.

FORTIFIED WINES

SPAIN

10 Palo Cortado Sherry 37.5cl **£6.25**

Dry' declares the label on this quite-outstanding sherry by Emilio Lustau. It is indeed dry – as all proper sherry is – and of the most marvellous sheeny conker colour, perfumed with all the preserved fruit and nut piquancy imaginable and piercingly pungent on the palate. As the label also boasts, this is a 'very rare' sherry – the palo cortado style is the trickiest of the solera range to summon up – and at the price (I paid just £5.50 on promo) very rare value too; 19% alcohol. Serve well-chilled in a proper small wine glass, and wonder at it.

Sainsbury's

It's all about the Taste the Difference range at Sainsbury's. As I had to buy all my samples this year – as in 2020 and 2021 because of the pestilence but in 2022 because Sainsbury's didn't invite me to their tasting – I stuck largely to the TTD wines and was rewarded with gratifying consistency.

And, of course, I limited myself to wines on promotion. Sainsbury's does very regular 25%-off-any-six (or more) offers, sometimes on top of discounts on individual wines, so I got some good deals. This is consumer journalism at its finest I reckon, but it's not exactly selfless as I continue to admire the Sainsbury's wine offering, however inhospitable they are at HQ.

Mind you, while there have been very few innovations in the wine line over these last difficult years, there are some alarming gaps opening up in the range. Old favourites missing this year include red wines TTD Barbaresco, TTD Pic St Loup and Paul Jaboulet Côtes du Rhône. I'm still mourning the loss of white TTD Greco di Tufo and Dr L Riesling.

And now it's rumoured that a foreign predator is stalking Sainsbury's. It's one of the private equity firms that was outbid for the Morrisons takeover, so presumably a serious contender. Whatever next?

RED WINES

FRANCE

8 Taste the Difference Languedoc Red 2020 £7.50

As dense and savoury as ever, this spicy generic Mediterranean winter wine by Jean-Paul Mas is a bit harder than the previous vintage; 13.5% alcohol. I tasted it in the spring; it might round out a bit for in-season enjoyment. Frequently discounted.

8 Taste the Difference St Chinian 2018 £9.00

Still on shelf from last year, a fine vintage of this upcountry Languedoc AP with lurid deep-purple colour, heady herby hot-bramble nose and trademark fruits-of-the-forest savour; 14.5% alcohol. I paid £6.75 on promo.

8 Taste the Difference Côtes du Ventoux 2019 £10.00

This darkly brambly and spicy Rhône neighbour centred on a notoriously exhausting windswept mountain on the Tour de France route is vivid and juicy in this glorious vintage; 14.5% alcohol. Thanks to a double promo, I got mine for £6.37.

9 Château Les Bouysses Cahors 2018 £13.00

Consistenty delicious malbec from the variety's natural home of Cahors in the Lot Valley; dark and succulent with sun-spiced ripe blackberry savours made silky in oak casks; 13.5% alcohol. From a splendid estate founded in 1230 by a gentleman rejoicing in the name Raymond de Lard, I rate this one of the best Cahors of them all. Frequently on useful discount.

RED WINES

FRANCE

8 **Taste the Difference Château de Pierreux Brouilly 2021 £14.00**

New departure for Sainsburys: a grand Beaujolais cru of succulent juiciness and bounce with labyrinthine slinky dark-fruit sensations, classic top-flight wine of the region at an appropriate price to seek out, particularly when on blanket promo at £10.50; 14.5% alcohol.

ITALY

10 **Taste the Difference Primitivo Puglia 2021 £7.00**

Utterly dependable bargain from Salento in the stiletto bit of Italy's 'heel' now known to tourists of Puglia as Trullo country. This is an excellent follow-up to the fine 2020 vintage and lighter in heft but full of dark spiciness for a humble IGT wine; 13.5% alcohol. Sainsbury's are forever discounting it to £6. I got mine for £4.50 in a 25%-off-six promo. Mad.

PORTUGAL

9 **Taste the Difference Douro 2019 £10.50**

The Douro had a pretty good harvest in 2019 but it has not been widely declared as a Port vintage – which I believe can mean more really good fruit is freed up for table wines. This one from Symington family estates, for instance. It's alluringly dark with porty richness and spicy, minty savours; 14% alcohol. It was on offer at £7.50 and it so happened a 25%-off-six promo was also in force, so I got my bottle for £5.70.

8 **Feuerheerd's Anchor Wine 2019 £11.00**

Dotty package – the bottle has a peculiar wrap-around label – this otherwise respectable Douro table wine is a real find. Solidly dark hue and unmistakably Port-llike on the nose, it has spent a year ageing in old Port casks. Slinky, nicely weighted, rich black fruit with warm spice, a very attractive wine; 13% alcohol. I paid £8 on promo.

RED WINES

SOUTH AFRICA

8 **Bruce Jack Fairtrade Shiraz 2020** £7.00

This Western Cape red from a considerable range marketed under the Bruce Jack brand seems underpriced, especially at occasional Sainsbury's promo price of £6. Wholesome whack of brambly-ripe juicy fruit and 14.5% alcohol. Proper barbecue wine.

SPAIN

9 **Taste the Difference Cepa Alegro Rioja Reserva 2015** £9.00

Sweet cassis and creamy vanilla advance on nose and tongue in seductive harmony from this really charming and wholesomely developed bargain from a famously ripe vintage; 13.5% alcohol.

8 **Taste the Difference Rioja Gran Reserva 2014** £13.50

Made by Cune/CVNE, it's just turning to orange at the rim and taking on a lacy delicacy on the palate but the sweet cassis fruit is standing up to the vanilla oak; 14% alcohol. It's more than academic pleasure to drink such an old wine at such a sensible price – thanks to two coeval promos I paid just £8.25.

WHITE WINES

FRANCE

Sainsbury's

10 Bouchard Aîné et Fils Chardonnay Réserve du Conseiller 2020 £8.00

Bouchard Aîné is a venerable Burgundy producer (est 1750) but this wine is not burgundy. The label bears the designation 'Vin de France', which means, as UK importer Matthew Clark helpfully puts it, that the wine 'is made in the Vin de France area of France'. I'm telling you all this because I really liked this peaches-and-cream/crisp-and-tangy 12.5% alcohol chardonnay and I don't care where it comes from. It's as good as most generic white burgundy and cheaper (I paid £7 on promo).

9 Taste the Difference Côtes du Rhône Blanc 2021 £8.00

I hope I will never tire of reporting on this brilliant concoction for Sainsbury's by top Rhône name Gabriel Meffre. Launched with the fabled 2015 vintage it's a crafty blend of grenache blanc, marsanne and vermentino (previous years have included roussanne and viognier) to make a gold-coloured, leesy, peachy and satifying dry white of complexity and heft; 12.5% alcohol. Tastes much more expensive than it is.

9 Vouvray La Couronne des Plantagenets 2020 £8.00

Lovely soft wine from one of the great appellations of the Loire Valley; honey-scented, sweetly ripe in a grapey (not a sugary) way and yet appley-fresh with a real citrus lift at the edge. Don't be put off by the designation demi-sec on the label 12% alcohol. This one's for you, Adrian.

WHITE WINES

FRANCE

8 **Taste the Difference Languedoc Blanc 2021 £8.00**
This peachy-appley, well-coloured, full-bottomed blend by Languedoc maestro Jean-Claude Mas is as lush as ever in what has been a difficult vintage; 13% alcohol. Price has drifted upwards but promos are still frequent.

8 **Taste the Difference Pouilly-Fumé 2020 £13.00**
Dependable sauvignon blanc from one of the Loire Valley's classic appellations, suitably river-pebble-fresh as well as lush, long and complex with grassy-nettly-herby nuance; 14% alcohol. Serious wine at a serious price.

ITALY

9 **Taste the Difference Trentino Chardonnay 2021 £8.50**
New wine! Not many of these this year, and it's a very welcome one. Trentino is Italy's northernmost wine region, sub-Alpine, and chardonnay is a grape little known anywhere in Italy let alone up here. But this is good, straw in colour and correspondingly ripe with sweet-apple fruit on nose and palate, enriched by a bit of oak contact I think, and with balancing mineral-citrus influences; 12.5% alcohol.

NEW ZEALAND

8 **Taste the Difference Coolwater Bay Sauvignon Blanc 2021 £8.00**
Awatere, Marlborough, wine by esteemed Yealands Estate, frankly peapod in its green appeal, lots of ripe grassiness with gooseberry and nettle in the savour; you get a lot of distinct Kiwi sauvignon style for your money; 13% alcohol.

WHITE WINES

SPAIN

8 Faustino Rivero Ulecia Albariño 2021 £13.00

The translucent ultramarine flute bottle is a wonder to behold and the wine is jolly good, seaside-fresh tangy white-fruit aromas and flavours, a proper Rias Baixas albariño that's easy to like; 12.5% alcohol. The price has lifted a bit but it's still a good buy.

SPARKLING WINES

FRANCE

9 Sainsbury's Demi-Sec Champagne £19.00

For celebrants who don't like their champagne too 'green' this well-made *demi-sec* (half-dry) wine is an inspired compromise. It is not at all sweet, but mellow and comforting as well as brisk and refreshing in the proper way; mature-tasting, you might say, with 12% alcohol. Why it is cheaper than Sainsbury's Blanc de Noir (see wine below for disturbing revelation) I cannot fathom.

5 Sainsbury's Blanc de Noirs Champagne Brut £21.00

Suddenly, a bottle that tasted suspiciously sweet, as if the sugar at the dosage stage has been overdone. Alarming. I am reserving judgement.

Tesco

Tesco was among the five retailers figuring in this book who invited me to taste their wine range this year. I got to the Co-op, Majestic, Marks & Spencer and Waitrose events in good order, as evidenced by the enthusiastic entries each has in this edition.

But I failed to make it to Tesco. As it was a problematic day for train travel (sound familiar?) I resolved on the only alternative, a bus from Somerset, where I live, to London, where all the tastings are invariably staged. The vehicle in question broke down at Stonehenge (where there are all sorts of breakdowns, I can assure you) and the operator left us passengers stranded. Unhappily, the tasting was organised on a time-slot basis due to Covid measures and I wasn't going to make it, so I rang home and my wife Sheila very kindly came and collected me for the melancholy return journey.

Tesco were kind too. I did ring to say I couldn't get there, and they were sympathetic. Later I was sent some samples to taste in consolation. Six bottles were a rather small fraction of the 140 opened at the tasting, but every little helps, as they say.

So, most of the reports that follow this are wines I bought in my nearest stores. In preparation for this kind of contingency during Covid I had acquired a Tesco Clubcard and must say it has been an extremely valuable aid to budget shopping.

It seems many, if not most, of Tesco's wine promotions are now targeted exclusively at Clubcard holders. I gather there are 17 million of them. And I'm not surprised.

I noticed in the late summer of 2022 that Tesco was introducing some really quite inspired new wines at what might be termed cost-of-living crisis prices. Outstanding among these is Vista Castelli Montepulciano d'Abruzzo which makes its last-minute appearance on page 90. The price is £4.75. It's crackingly good in its way, definitely merits maximum score, and to say it's good value for money is rather to understate the case.

I am rather hoping that Tesco is reacting early to the inevitable exigencies of the crisis by seriously boosting the choice of affordable wines on offer. The new launches, for example, include claret, Côtes du Rhône and both red and white Rioja all at £5. Tesco is a strong performer in the mid-price wine range, and I have great hopes too for its performance in economy class.

RED WINES

FRANCE

9 Tesco Beaujolais 2020 **£5.00**

This marvellous wine, featured annually in these pages for more than a decade, is now in *memoriam*. Tesco confirmed to me at time of going to press they were 'de-listing' it for reasons not given and selling off the last of the stock at £3.85 a bottle. A sad exit for the best Beaujolais bargain in Britain. I am mentioning it here in case vigilant readers find any lingering leftovers in local branches, but this is really just a sentimental farewell.

8 Tesco French Malbec 2020 **£5.00**

It's generic Midi wine but reportedly comes from favoured biodynamic vineyards in the Cahors region. Likeable and quite profound gently spiced hedgerow red with wholesome grip; 13% alcohol.

8 Finest Malbec Cahors 2020 **£7.50**

You might think it slight, far from the 'black wine' of Cahors legend, but this does have substance and grip as well as gently spicy blackberry fruit; 13.5% alcohol. The modern packaging in a screwcap bottle seems at odds with the fogeyish appeal of Cahors, but worth a try anyway.

8 Côtes du Rhône Villages M Chapoutier 2020 **£9.50**

Finely weighted elegant CdR from one of the region's great names (Chapoutier was founded in 1808); relatively light in colour and heft in this vintage but firmly focused in its redcurrant-blackberry fruit with trademark pepper trace and keen edge; 14.5% alcohol.

RED WINES

ITALY

Tesco

10 Vista Castelli Montepulciano d'Abruzzo 2020 £4.75

Tesco has always done a good line in bargain Montepulciano and this is the best ever. It's plump, juicy and wholesomely ripe (12.5% alcohol) with grippy cherry and hedgerow-fruit savour. The price is ridiculous.

8 Melini Chianti Governo 2020 £9.00

Distinctly blue theme to the labelling of this odd skittle-shaped bottle, maybe recalling the old days when Chianti was commonly produced by the governo method of adding weight and colour.

10 Belpasso Vino Rosso 2019 £10.00

Made by Allegrini, one of the great names of Verona, a pioneer of organic viticulture and leading light of Valpolicella, this wine is a ripasso, pitch-dark, intense crimson in colour, blooming violet-cassis mint aroma and darkly intense black fruit with tea-like tannic grip perfectly judged to balance the lush ripeness; 13.5% alcohol. I paid £6.75 on a particularly fortuitous Clubcard day but would have willingly handed over the tenner.

8 Castello Banfi Rosso di Montalcino 2020 £17.00

Banfi is a manicured resort-hotel-cum-vineyard enterprise centred on a spectacular castellated property in the Tuscan hilltown of Montalcino, home to the renowned and expensive wine Brunello di Montalcino. This wine is from sangiovese (Chianti) grapes rather than brunello (a sangiovese clone) and is middling in weight (though 14.5% alcohol) with good regional savour.

RED WINES

PORTUGAL

8 Finest Douro 2019 — **£10.00**

Nicely balanced wine from Port country has the right deep-crimson colour and heady suggestion of the fortified wine on the nose, attractively silky-minty black fruit and lingering aftertaste; 13% alcohol. Look for the 18th-century illustration on the label; don't confuse it with the plain Tesco Douro.

SOUTH AFRICA

8 The Misfits Cinsault 2021 — **£9.00**

Cryptically named varietal from Western Cape's Ken Forrester, handsomely ruby in colour and intriguingly scented of leafy redcurrant. It's light in weight but focused and mineral in its pure-fruit, berry/plum savour; 12.5% alcohol. Would be a good match for rich fish cookery as well as poultry and game. The name is a mystery – don't let it put you off.

SPAIN

9 Finest Rioja Reserva Viña del Cura 2017 — **£9.00**

Robust cassis-packed creamily oaked new vintage of this old favourite is quite fiery in its ripeness but should round out nicely given time; 14.5% alcohol. The 2017 Rioja harvest was a difficult one, thanks to late frosts in spring and drought in summer. Buy this vintage now while stocks last, especially at the 25% off I got with my Clubcard.

PINK WINES

FRANCE

8 Love by Léoube 2021 — **£15.00**

Delicate pale colour is shown off to full advantage in the clear bottle with arty painted-on self-conscious name and little else. It's a particularly crisp and bright-tasting Côtes de Provence rosé, although if I tasted it without seeing the colour I doubt I would guess it was anything other than white wine. It is made, however, entirely from organically grown black-skinned grapes grenache and cinsault, presumably only momentarily left in contact with the skins before run-off. Conscientiously produced and really rather good, which it needs to be at the price; 13% alcohol.

WHITE WINES

ARGENTINA

8 **DV Catena Chardonnay Historico 2019** **£12.00**

Elegant minerally Mendoza wine with bright brassica-grapefruit crispness happily partnered with lushly ripe apple-sweet fruit. Tasting this on Channel 4 show *Sunday Brunch*, I was impressed when presenter Simon Rimmer compared its flintiness to the usually-inimitable style of Chablis. A distinctive wine from century-old Uco Valley vineyards (thus the 'historico' in the name); 13.5% alcohol. DV Catena was Domingo Vicente of that ilk, who in 1934 married Angelica Zapata, launching a dynasty that has done much to propel Argentina into the first division of world winemaking.

AUSTRALIA

8 **Taparoo Chardonnay 2021** **£4.25**

Look at the price. How do they do it? It's probably shipped in bulk and bottled in the UK but it's daisy fresh, recognisable crisp-apple chardy and clean as whistle; 12.5% alcohol.

8 **Petaluma Chardonnay 2018** **£16.00**

Grand Adelaide Hills wine, lemon-gold in colour and expensively scented of white peaches and elusive vanilla; long lush fruit but really quite restrained in the modern Aussie manner; 13.5% alcohol.

WHITE WINES

CHILE

8 Cono Sur Bicicleta Viognier 2021 £6.00

This reliable and reliably good-value brand owned by redoubtable Concha y Toro has the aromatic preserved-apricot and floral style you hope for from viognier, and easy acidity to balance; 13.5% alcohol. If I remember right the bicycle theme is virtue signalling of the means of transport employed in the vineyards.

FRANCE

9 Finest St Mont 2019 £7.00

Still on shelf from last year, 2019 is a terrific vintage for this annual favourite from Producteurs Plaimont in Gascony. Autumn-gold colour, sweet floral aromas, fruits encompassing apple and pear along with melon and mango – a proper basket of fresh-fruit flavours, brisk and bright; 13.5% alcohol.

ITALY

8 Finest Soave Superiore Classico 2020 £7.50

I was tempted into trying this by a rave review in a national newspaper. It failed on first taste to live up to expectations but a day later turned out tangy-peachy in the approved Soave manner with the hallmark lick of creamy blanched almond to balance the citrus; good colour and heft at 13% alcohol.

SOUTH AFRICA

9 Finest Stellenbosch Chenin Blanc 2021 £7.50

Excellent balance of honey-hinting stone fruit and lively lemon lift in this perennial favourite from Fairtrade winery Stellenrust; Cape chenin blanc is firmly establishing itself as one of the world's most distinctive white-wine styles, refreshing, satisfying, thought-provoking; 13.5% alcohol. Good value, this one.

WHITE WINES

SOUTH AFRICA

9 Vergelegen Sauvignon Blanc 2021 £10.00

Lush Stellenbosch wine from one of the region's premier estates in classic full-fruit Cape style evoking gooseberry and pea-shoot, seagrass and citrus. There's 5% semillon in the mix, in the Bordeaux sauvignon style, and I do believe it adds a little tropical lavishness; 13.5% alcohol.

8 Stellenbosch Manor Barrel-Fermented Chenin Blanc 2020 £14.00

Special-occasion wine from Stellenrust, who make Tesco's own Cape chenin blanc – *see* page 93. This one's entirely fermented in oak casks and has corresponding plumpness in its exotic aromas and fruit, taking in notions of peach and apricot, blanched almond and twangy citrus at the edge, in the best chenin blanc tradition. You do notice this is special – a good and versatile food wine: fish or fowl, salads and charcuterie; 14% alcohol.

FORTIFIED WINES

PORTUGAL

10 Finest Ten-Year-Old Tawny Port £12.50

The original ruby hue is just moving to the copper-amber colour known to the Port trade as tawny and the 'marriage' of the 77% alcohol neutral spirit with the heady wine has settled down very comfortably into a union of luscious sweetness with defined spicy-nutty-figgy savour; 20% alcohol. I think this is the best-value Port of its type on the market, not just for drinking after dinner but as a fine aperitif served straight from the fridge.

SPARKLING WINES

ENGLAND

8 Finest English Sparkling Brut £21.00
Made by the irresistibly named Hush Heath estate in Kent it's from standard champagne grapes and made using the champagne method. It's a fully-fizzy dry wine, crisp and with a little bready richness from the yeast in the fermentation, appley and fresh; 12% alcohol. I like it but at the same price as Tesco's own-label champagne, it's not a bargain.

FRANCE

9 Finest 1531 Blanquette de Limoux Brut 2020 £9.50
New vintage of this sterling perennial from the Pyrenees. This is a very busily foaming and fresh sparkling wine, crisp and refreshing, and an improvement on several tyro champagnes I can think of; 12.5% alcohol. And look at the price.

10 Finest Premier Cru Champagne Brut £21.00
By a distance, my preferred supermarket own-label champagne. The clue might be in the designation Premier Cru, applying to the status of the source vineyards in the region's Cotes des Blancs. Humbler champagnes as a rule do not come from there. Significantly, this wine has a fine colour, warm bakery whiff and crisp fruits in a rush of busy mousse to a clean end flavour; 12.5% alcohol. Half-bottles available at £12.

ITALY

8 Franciacorta Castel Fagia Extra Brut £15.50
Franciacorta is Italy's forgotten fizz. It's made in Brescia, Lombardy, by the same method as champagne, largely from chardonnay grapes (again as in champagne) and can aspire to fizzy heights. This one certainly does, with its gold colour, full persistent mousse and apple-crisp flavours, genuinely interesting and refreshing with 12.5% alcohol. Thank you, Magali Bellego, for reminding me of what we have been missing.

Waitrose

There are about 1200 wines on Waitrose's list, and I have tasted a lot of them, both as a fortunate invitee to this year's expansive press tasting and as an eager customer in my local store. Very many of these wines are extremely good and sensible value. Most are not sold in any other supermarket, even though few of Waitrose's wines are 'own-label'.

The upshot is that this entry is by far the most extensive in this book. There are 80 wines recommended. I would add more but there isn't space. And I know not everybody shops at Waitrose.

If you're not a Waitrose customer, please consider this: Waitrose is truly competitive in price. Promotional discounts are perpetual on dozens of wines on a changing month-by-month basis, and from time to time there is a comprehensive 25 per cent off the entire range if you buy six or more bottles, any mix. These deals usually last just a week. And Waitrose is the only retailer still giving 5 per cent off if you buy any six bottles at once, any time.

But the main attraction is, of course, the sheer quality and diversity. As you will see from the following lengthy listing, there's much to choose from. One innovation I'd like to point out is a new own-label range called 'Loved & Found'. It's an endearing collection of wines from unexpected places, and many of them are expectedly good.

RED WINES

ARGENTINA

10 Tilimuqui Organic Malbec 2021 £11.99

I paid £7.99 in what seemed to me a rashly generous promo. Loved the sheeny violet-crimson blood-opaque colour and luxuriant new-picked sun-baked blackberry-blackcurrant aroma; the silky texture and intense corresponding fruit live up entirely to the promise in a young wine that suggests longer maturation than it's had, and a higher price tag even than the full-ticket. It's 13% alcohol – modest for a wine of this origin and ripeness. A proper flag-flyer for the Fairtrade scheme (producer co-op La Riojana is a leading participant) and for Argentina.

9 Clos de los Siete 2019 £16.99

Enduring Mendoza brand, half malbec plus a medley in descending proportion of merlot, syrah, cab sauvignon, cab franc and petit verdot. I'm telling you all this because it appears to be a magic formula. The wine is coal dark, gorgeously intense with berry fruits and creamy oak influence and sublimely balanced for ridiculously easy drinking; 14.5% alcohol. Utterly seductive.

AUSTRALIA

8 Farm Hand Organic Merlot 2020 £9.99

This is merlot with a bit of edge – gentle tannin rimming the sweetly ripe black-cherry fruit. It works well, balancing ripeness and briskness to show off the undoubted merits (perhaps not always realised) of the grape variety; 14.5% alcohol.

RED WINES

AUSTRALIA

8 Elephant in the Room Palatial Pinot Noir 2021 £10.99

I don't know why Aussie winemakers resort to gimmicky names and it doesn't put me off this charming, pale but plump pinot perfumed with ripe English cherries (yes, English, really) with softness of texture but real definition of fruit; 13.5% alcohol. It's artful and quite remarkable really.

8 Little Giant Barossa Shiraz 2020 £12.99

Deep maroon colour to this pleasing bumper food wine manifests in lush, warm but very nicely weighted black fruits; it's positively restrained in its delivery; 14.5% alcohol.

9 Shaw + Smith Shiraz 2018 £31.00

This classic Adelaide Hills wine is a big gripper with pomegranate and spicy redcurrant highlights to the sincerely ripe and balanced savoury shiraz. Hefty but poised, sumptuous from new-oak contact, but very trim at the finish; 14% alcohol. Would suit a very special occasion – maybe a sporting toast to England recovering The Ashes – soon or, admittedly, far in the future. Waitrose Cellar only.

CHILE

8 Miguel Torres Digno Pais 2020 £7.99

A healthy, juicy red wine with 13% alcohol comparable to Beaujolais – made by the same method of carbonic maceration from a grape variety said to have been brought to Chile 500 years ago by Cortés, no less. Catalan hero Miguel Torres, something of a pioneer himself – but much nicer than Cortés – makes this wine in tribute to Chile's great and growing place on the world wine map.

RED WINES

FRANCE

8 Sous le Soleil du Midi Merlot 2021 £5.99
Naff-looking package lets down this likeable beetroot-hued Languedoc pure varietal with a sweetly inviting black-cherry nose and ripe plump black fruit, well-trimmed for a clean finish; 13.5% alcohol. Keen bargain.

8 Waitrose Loved & Found Caladoc 2021 £7.49
Caladoc's the grape's name, a cross between grenache and malbec. Who knew? I suppose that's what qualifies this likeable Languedoc wine for Waitrose's new Loved & Found range. It's quite light to look at, a cheery purple in colour and bouncing with brambly fruit, clean-finishing and uplifting; 13.5% alcohol.

9 Château Capendu La Comelle Corbières 2019 £7.99
A Languedoc vineyard lately acquired by regional wine wizard Jean-Claude Mas provides this unexpectedly light-coloured but beguilingly ripe blend of carignan, grenache and syrah. Mediterranean herbs illuminate the substantial, discreetly creamy blackberry savours, and I like it a lot; 14% alcohol.

8 Blueprint Beaujolais Villages 2019 £7.99
Very decent, lively-juicy bouncing pure-fruit wine not at all inhibited by its relative senility; 13.5% alcohol. Made by Georges Duboeuf for Waitrose's rather spartan own-label range, it's a much better bet than the consistently dull and overpriced Cuvée des Vignerons Beaujolais AC at £7.79.

RED WINES

FRANCE

8 **Paul Mas Réserve Languedoc Rouge 2020** **£9.39**

Extravagant embossed bottle delivers a suitably opulent regional blend of grenache, syrah and carignan from Languedoc legend Jean-Claude Mas, here contriving a stout but silky blackly intense cold-weather red of spicy savour with 14% alcohol. Impressive, especially at £7.04 on promo.

8 **Gabriel Meffre Organic Côtes du Rhône 2020** **£10.69**

Grandly packaged in an embossed bottle with incongruous screwcap closure, a wholesomely rich, blackly spicy and robust classic CdR from a famously fortuitous vintage in the region; 14.5% alcohol. I paid £8.02 on promo.

9 **Cairanne Réserve des Hospitalières Cru des Côtes du Rhône 2019** **£11.99**

Bold but defined superior Côtes du Rhône with deep crimson hue, plum and liquorice wafts and spicy black fruits, benefitting from a bit of time in bottle (assuming you've got the 2019, which was still listed as we went to press); 14.5% alcohol. A bargain at the regular promo price of £8.99.

8 **Brouilly Domaine Tavian 2021** **£12.99**

This vivid Beaujolais cru has depth of colour and fruit with plenty of juicy bounce; it will no doubt develop in the bottle as these pricey wines are supposed to, but it's already rather delicious; 12.5% alcohol.

RED WINES

FRANCE

8 Château La Raze Beauvallet 2015 £14.99
It's a cru bourgeois from the Médoc, home to grand cru classé estates churning out bottles at £100 apiece, and you get something of the flavour at the £9.99 I paid on offer. Elegant ruby colour showing a shade of orange (2015 vintage, remember) and sleek, balanced fruits though no oak, slight laciness of age; 13% alcohol. Fun.

9 Château Carcanieux 2010 £16.00
Another cru bourgeois from the Médoc (see Ch La Raze Beauvallet above) and this time really quite old. Made by grand Bordeaux négoçiant-propriétaire Ginestet, it has fine ruby colour, sweet cassis aroma and bright silky blackcurrant fruit with good grip, very proper claret sleek with new-oak contact, I'd say; 13% alcohol. Cheap for what it is, really, and a rare chance from a supermarket to try the real thing.

8 Clos St Michel Châteauneuf du Pape 2019 £24.99
Outrageously expensive (though I paid £19.99 on promo) as a special buy for an extra-special occasion but a safe bet, this was reassuringly opaque and developed in colour with a saucily sweet nose and silky vanilla-enriched discreetly spicy typical fruit; 14% alcohol. If you just have to have a CdP, this one is more honest and better value than most I have tried of late.

RED WINES

ITALY

10 **Waitrose Loved and Found Perricone 2020** **£7.99**
Sicilian country wine absolutely bouncing with brambly juiciness and plump ripeness. It's cheap for this quality – and I paid just £6 on promo. Picnic wine certainly and it will serve very well from the fridge; 13.5% alcohol. Perricone is a grape variety apparently native to the northeastern part of the island and grown in very small quantities. More please.

8 **Waitrose Loved and Found Frappato 2021** **£7.99**
New wine for the new range is from Sicily, pale in colour, rose-petal-like perfume, fresh juicy redcurranty fruit that might tempt a spell in the fridge; 13.5% alcohol. Quirky lunchtime and party red.

10 **Borgodei Trulli Salice Salentino 2020** **£8.99**
Terrific new vintage for this consistently delectable Puglian negroamaro is dense in texture but poised in weight, wildly savoury in its blackberry-blueberry fruit and perfectly taut at the edge; 13.5% alcohol. Extraordinary wine at a very fair price, and yet quite often on promo at £6.99.

10 **Terre de Faiano Primitivo 2021** **£9.99**
This Puglian organic wine with unmistakable orange-coloured label is a phenomenon. Made by the Appassimento method, it seems almost perpetually on promotion, at or sometimes below £7.99. Gloriously dark and rich chocolatey-spicy brambly-ripe food red (all pasta and carnivorous menus) with perfectly judged briskness at the finish; 13.5% alcohol.

RED WINES

ITALY

9 **Araldica Barbera d'Asti Superiore 2019** **£9.99**
Sleek and stylish Piedmont speciality from a big but admirable corporate producer; impressive crimson colour, lively intense violet and cassis nose and sleek, racy black fruit; distinctive and purposeful as a match for sticky pasta but also for savoury fish dishes and chicken or duck; 14.5% alcohol. Regularly discounted to £7.49.

9 **Montidori Sangiovese 2020** **£9.99**
The dumpy bottle is a bit disconcerting but this sangiovese (the grape of Chianti) from the region of Emilia-Romagna is gratifyingly generous and plump with a lovely intense crimson colour, blackberry/sour-cherry aromas and matching fruit, fortified with must from dried grapes, ripasso-style; 13.5% alcohol. A curiosity from a region known only for one other wine, Lambrusco, but a very likeable one. I paid £7.99 on promo.

8 **Pazzia Primitivo di Manduria 2020** **£11.99**
Looking alluring behind its bold stripy label this seductive cushiony-plump Puglian pasta red has sweetly ripe blackberry fruit and charming violet scents and flavours – a truly generous and amenable wine regularly on promo at around £9; 14% alcohol.

9 **Masi Campofiorin Rosso di Verona 2018** **£12.99**
Valpolicella variant with the generous sour-cherry fruit of the base wine, bumped up with a warmly plummy-cinnamon-violet-marzipan boost of concentrate from part-dried must to make a fine marriage of savours and textures; 13% alcohol. Paid £9.99 on promo – a gift.

RED WINES

ITALY

Waitrose

0 Terredora di Paolo Aglianico 2019 £12.99
A really nasty, tainted and weedy Campania wine. Maybe a bad bottle, but othwerwise, Waitrose has no business listing it. Attractive label, but I was alerted by the horrible polymer 'cork' and saddened by the bitter nature of the wine.

8 Collemassari Rosso Riserva Montecucco 2018 £14.99
From Tuscany, home of Chianti, and made mostly with sangiovese, the grape of Chianti, this isn't Chianti, but a big, plump meat and cheese red with some of the Chianti sour-cherry abrasion to it, and a lot of intense coffee and warm spice savour besides; long and satisfying and 15% alcohol.

7 Terre di Faiano Rosso Organic 2021 2.25l £25.99
This is not the same wine as the orange-labelled Terre di Faiano Primitivo that wins a top score (again) elsewhere in this edition. It's from the same producer but is negroamaro-based and in a whopping cylindrical bag-in box construct that is difficult to open and operate (I have witnesses). The wine is okay, darkly fruity with chocolate and caramel notes; 13.5% alcohol. Price is equivalent to £8.66 per bottle.

RED WINES

ITALY

9 Masi Costasera Amarone Classico 2016 £34.99

Tasted out of curiosity – £35 wines are not really my stock in trade – this was worth the trouble. Made by Valpolicella virtuoso Masi it appears gloopy dense but is light on its feet with a mature-looking alluring ruby hue, dark roasty scents and flavours with notes of coffee, chocolate and preserved fruits, the right abrasion of the amarone (it means 'bitter') from the Appassimento method and a tight but sumptuously lingering finish; 15% alcohol. This is a top wine in its class and Waitrose clearly rate it. In spite of the price, they have in 2022 increased the number of stores stocking it from 9 to 139.

NEW ZEALAND

8 Astrolabe Pinot Noir 2018 £18.99

This grand Marlborough wine has limpid pale proper pinot colour and seductive sweet-cherry/raspberry scent translating into restrained but luscious slinky fruit with earthy ripeness; nice buy even at this price; 13.5% alcohol.

SOUTH AFRICA

8 Kanonkop Kadette Pinotage 2019 £12.99

Stellenbosch stalwart; soupy-spicy blackcurrant savours with creamy slink and happily contrasting hint of tar – distinctive wine from the Cape's own indigenous grape; 14% alcohol.

RED WINES

SPAIN

8 Igo Organic Red Wine Can 2019 £3.99

This Navarra wine is what it says on the tin: wine. And I tasted it. Not bad. Healthy red-fruit nose, bright even juicy strawberry-redcurrant clean fruit; 14% alcohol. As I say, not bad, but not cheap either at equivalent to £12 for a standard 75cl bottle.

7 Castillo de Olite Colleccion 2015 £8.99

Still on shelf from last year this 2015 vintage is showing its age, tasting even less substantial than when I tasted it a year earlier and noted it was measurably less intense than the preceding vintage. If you find a later vintage of this likeable cassis-sweet but balanced long-oaked Navarra, I still recommend giving it a try; 13.5% alcohol.

9 Celler de Capçanes Lasendal Sellecció 2019 £10.99

Attractive package, grenache and syrah from D0 Monsant, Catalan neighbour to cult Priorat. Slinky and sleek balsamic redcurrant-bright fruit delicate in weight but firm and full; distinctive, memorable with Mama's spiffy duck lunch; 14.5% alcohol. I paid about £8 on promo – great value.

8 Baron de Ley Club Privado Reserva Rioja 2017 £12.99

New variation from estimable Baron de Ley is all tempranillo: strong cassis flavours tempered by sweet vanilla with a good grip; 14.5% alcohol. Memorable wine that should develop for years.

RED WINES

SPAIN

9 La Petite Agnès Priorat 2019 £14.99

In succession to last year's lavish 2017, a gorgeous new vintage for this brooding garnacha-led spicy-mineral intense blackberry-pie smoothie from Catalonia's most arcane (and pricey) vineyard backwater, Priorat; it's 15% alcohol but all-too easy to drink, silkily oaked, supple and gripping. Will evolve in bottle for years and years. I paid £11.24 on promo.

PINK WINES

FRANCE

8 L'Arène des Anges Rosé Costières de Nîmes 2021 £7.99

New label design – an improvement – for this stalwart grenache-based Languedoc pink but the same dependable bold colour, generous bright strawberry-apple juicy crispness and freshness of savour; nicely made dry wine; 13% alcohol.

8 Le Bijou de Sophie Valrose Rosé 2021 £10.99

The fine pale delicate colour to this delightful dry but generously fruity pink wine from the Coteaux de Béziers is not its only attraction. Endearing strawberry traces in a crisp medium of pink-tasting refreshingness; 12.5% alcohol. Sophie Valrose was a winemaker in the region long ago who stood up for quality – and for the rights of women workers.

Waitrose

PINK WINES

ITALY

8 **La Cerisa Rosa Pinot Grigio Rosé 2021** **£8.49**

As a great enthusiast neither of pink wines or pinot grigio I surprised myself somwhat by liking this concoction from Lombardy. It's pretty pale with a dry entry, but blooms into a positive party of trim alpine-strawberry savour, pleasingly fresh and lively; 12.5% alcohol.

WHITE WINES

AUSTRALIA

8 **Yalumba Organic Viognier 2021** **£9.99**

Looks, smells and tastes wholesomely ripe as viognier should, with trademark apricot, nectarine and melon notes very nicely balanced out with the citrus twang at the finish; 13.5% alcohol. Nice drinks-party white as well as a match for fish and fowl.

8 **Yering Station The Elms Chardonnay 2021** **£10.49**

Sounding as if it's made in a care home (isn't The Elms the number one name for these establishments, even in *The Archers*?) this Victoria-state wine displays creditably old-fashioned virtues: creamy apple-pie style with lifting citrus edge to the long, comforting savour; 13% alcohol.

8 **Elephant in the Room Prodigious Pinot Gris 2021** **£10.99**

That they're calling it pinot gris as distinct from the more-populist pinot grigio is a good sign. You get the smoky element in the limey apple/pear fruit and plenty of refreshment from the zingy acidity; decent and interesting dry aperitif white or Asian-food match; 12% alcohol.

WHITE WINES

CHILE

8 **MontGras De-Vine Reserva Chardonnay 2021 £9.49**

Intriguing combo of brassica crispness and sweet-apple and mango ripeness in this artfully balanced and wholesome part-oaked and tangy-finishing dry wine; 13% alcohol.

FRANCE

9 **Waitrose Loved & Found Clairette 2020 £7.99**

The clairette grapes of the Languedoc tend to pop up in the region's perky sparkling wines, but here's a still one, made by star local producer Jean-Claude Mas. It really is a find: burgeoning with orchard fruit and elderflower, wholesomely ripe and crisply dry; 12.5% alcohol. Good match for fish dishes, charcuterie, you name it.

8 **Le Sauvignon Blanc de Balthazar 2021 £7.99**

Languedoc-made but rather more in the Loire Valley sauvignon style with its jolly grassy and tangy aromas and flavours; 12.5% alcohol.

8 **Coteaux du Layon Domaine des Forges St Aubin 2020 50cl £9.99**

Nectar. Lovely balanced aperitif or pudding wine with honeyed nose and luscious fruit in ideal balance; 12.5% alcohol. Serve very well chilled.

8 **Gérard Bertrand Naturae Chardonnay 2021 £9.99**

A 'natural' wine from Languedoc giant Gérard Bertrand (ex French international rugby star) made without sulphur products. It's a healthy colour (not orange), apple-sweet, crisp, refreshing and chardonnay-like and wholesome; 12.5% alcohol.

WHITE WINES

FRANCE

10 Wolfberger Alsace Pinot Blanc 2020 £10.99
Pinot blanc is unfashionable, but this one's perfect. It comes in a fat bottle instead of the customary Alsace flûte and further grabs the attention with its gorgeous gold colour and blossomy-white-nut perfume. The fruit is flush with the distinct vegetal green savours of PB, hinting at smokiness and even tropical fruit, all tidied up crisply in the ideal acidity at the finish; 12.5% alcohol. Top buy.

9 Alsace Riesling Kleinfels 2020 £10.99
This tastes more of Alsace than it does of riesling: dramatically perfumed with smoky white fruits in the style of pinot blanc or even gris, the main riesling clue is the raciness, even steeliness of the citrussy savour. Untypical, but arrestingly good and refreshing, a serious food matcher (anything) and a rare treat; 12.5% alcohol.

GERMANY

8 Weinhaus Pinot Gris Urmeer 2021 £7.99
From the Rheinhessen, but this fine, full smoky just-dry wine tastes more in an austere Alsace style than in the German; either way, it's lovely, with a tiny prickle of condition; 12.5% alcohol.

8 Weinhaus Sauvignon Blanc Kalkstein 2020 £9.99
Get this – Rhine sauvignon! Full of eager natural-tasting ripeness, it's a sort of sauvignon spätlese with easily recognisable gooseberry-nettly zest; 12.4% alcohol.

ITALY

8 Maree d'Ione Fiano 2021 £8.99
Intense but brightly refreshing peachy-ripe nutty-creamy organically produced dry Puglian white from ancient-origin fiano grape; 12.5% alcohol.

WHITE WINES

ITALY

8 Terre di Vita Pinot Grigio 2020 £8.99
From Sicily, it might be the extra sunshine that gives this organically produced PG an edge over the usual NE Italian style: pleasing colour, ripe orchard fruits, suggestions of smoke and spice, well-judged twang of citrus at the edge; 12.5% alcohol.

8 Forza della Natura Orange Catarratto 2021 £9.99
Yes, a natural wine, made without sulphur products, slightly orange-coloured and a little murky with a faint prickle, but pleasing and interesting nonetheless. Organically produced in Sicily, it's dry, fresh and fun; 12.5% alcohol.

9 Tre Fiori Greco di Tufo 2021 £10.99
It's probably my imagination, but tasting this wine from the Campania region inland from Naples strongly evokes the ancient volcanic nature of the landscape, as the tufo – soil evolved from eruptions over countless millennia – inoculates the flavours with something akin to brimstone. In short this is a fleetingly spicy dry white but also lush with exotic fruit and lifted by nectarine perfume and juiciness, very crisp at the end; 13% alcohol. Great match for creamy/eggy pasta dishes as well as fish and fowl.

8 Terranuova Gavi di Gavi 2021 £14.99
This big-flavoured Piedmont classic has green lushness and vivid white-fruit freshness, a top-of-the-range example of a currently trendy wine; 13% alcohol. If you're a fan, the price seems fair.

WHITE WINES

ITALY

9 **Santa Cristina Vin Santo Valdichiana Toscana 2016 50cl £17.49**

Rare and delicious Tuscan speciality wine from long-dried grapes; beautifully coloured – akin to amontillado sherry – with pure nutty-raisiny/grapey richness in fine balance; 12.5% alcohol. Served well-chilled with cantucci or similar.

NEW ZEALAND

8 **Crux Marlborough Sauvignon Blanc 2021 £10.49**

Sherbetty-prickly-fresh food wine that might be a bit much for aperitif sipping but a fine match for prawns off the barbie, or anything else off the barbie for that matter. Masses of mouthfilling sweet-pepper and sea-grass freshness, full of proper Kiwi SB zest; 12.5% alcohol. The name Crux stands for the great constellation of the antipodean heavens, the Southern Cross.

9 **Ara Single Estate Sauvignon Blanc 2021 £10.99**

The great big gooseberry-grassy blast on the nose of this serious Marlborough wine leads into familiar Kiwi flavours with lychee and new-hay lushness; memorable and a bargain at the £7.99 I paid on promo; 12% alcohol.

8 **Blind River Sauvignon Blanc 2021 £10.99**

The brisk and nettly entry reveals pleasingly intense lush-grassy middle flavours in a very jolly journey through the Awatere Valley (what a refreshing-sounding name that is for a stretch of vineyards) of Marlborough; 13% alcohol.

WHITE WINES

NEW ZEALAND

9 Yealands Reserve Grüner Veltliner 2021 £12.99

Kiwi spin on the rightly popular Austrian theme of aromatic GV; bright with crisp orchard fruits, counterpointed by ripe nectar notes in the plump body; standout fascinating, quite delicious; 13% alcohol. I paid £9.99 on promo.

SOUTH AFRICA

9 Reyneke Organic Chenin Blanc 2021 £9.99

Discreet honey-lemon counterpoint on the nose is followed up faithfully by a brilliantly contrived balance of nectary but zesty flavours in this fine aperitif wine (versatile with delicate menus too, I'd say); lovely freshness; 13% alcohol.

8 Boschendal Chardonnay 2020 £10.99

A big brand on good form; impressively ripe with melon alongside the proper chardonnay apple sweetness, conveyed in a buttery (outmoded term but fair enough here) oak-aided richness; jolly well-balanced and likeable; 13.5% alcohol.

8 Springfield Estate Special Cuvee Sauvignon Blanc 2021 £13.99

The attractive fruit-blossom bloom on this posh Robertson wine introduces a full, leesy, even luxuriant green-fruit grassy/nettly sauvignon bordering on the rich but in no sense sweet; attention-grabbing, piercingly defined, lovely stuff; 12.5% alcohol.

WHITE WINES

10 **Waitrose Loved & Found Treixadura 2021 £8.99**
Treixadura, pronounced something like 'tray-sha-doora', is a Portuguese grape mostly planted as a blending variety in vinho verde country, but this is a 100% treixadura from Galicia, better-known for its albariño. It's fascinating. 'Austere or extravagant?' I queried in my note. Well, try to imagine a meeting point. It's very full-flavoured with ripe-apple and sweet-pear plumpness balanced by citrus zing in a very defined acidity; 12% alcohol. Makes a distinct impression – highly commended.

9 **Beronia Rueda Verdejo 2020 £8.99**
Thoroughly dependable, excitingly fresh and rewarding dry wine from the rightly admired Rueda region (neighbour to esteemed Ribera del Duero). Well-coloured, assertive peachy-rancio perfume and vivacious grassy lushness all the way to the ideal citrus edge; 13% alcohol. Spain's answer to sauvignon and a worthy contender. I paid just £6.74 on promo.

8 **Baron de Ley Rioja 2020 £8.99**
Pale but interesting green-herbaceous-smoky dry white with good heft (12.5% alcohol) leaning more towards the long-lost oxidative style of Rioja blanco than to the modern zingy spin. Very plain presentation with screwcap but plenty of nuance, by trustworthy bodega Baron de Ley.

8 **Lagar de Cervera Albariño Rias Baixas 2021 £14.99**
Intense, leesy and long textbook wine from the wild Atlantic coast of Galicia; satisfying and stimulating; 12.5% alcohol. Sound investment.

SPARKLING WINES

ENGLAND

8 **Camel Valley Pinot Noir Rosé Brut** **£36.00**

Very pale copper colour, discreet strawberry whiff and briskness of mousse as well as delicate soft-fruit flavours combine cohesively to justify the price of this splendid Cornish contrivance; 12.5% alcohol.

FRANCE

8 **Ayala Brut Majeur Champagne Brut** **£29.99**

Almost fiercely lemony attack to the finely bubbled flavours of this warmly yeasty and obliging champagne. It stood out among the many famous names I tasted on the day; 12% alcohol.

WALES

8 **Glyndwr Brut 2019** **£21.99**

Welsh Regional Quality Sparkling Wine, it says on the label, and that's a fair description. It's from a vineyard established as long ago as 1982 and named after the last Welsh prince of Wales, known to the English as Owen Glendower, who is thought to have lived until about 1415 after conducting a long, heroic and doomed campaign for independence. The wine's a nice colour with a coppery hue, the fizz is busy and lasting and the fruit strawberry scented with a grapefruit element, fresh and distinctive; 12% alcohol.

FORTIFIED WINES

9 A Blend of Amontillado Medium Dry Sherry £7.69

As well as the cumbersome label description of this sublime 'Blueprint' own-label sherry by Sanchez-Romate, the bottle also bears a sticker proclaiming a bronze award from the 2017 International Wine Challenge. Bronze? The only thing bronze about this wine is in possible deference to its beautiful conker colour. Otherwise, it's pure gold, autumn aromas, fruits and sensations, 18.5% alcohol. Keep it refrigerated. I paid a laughable £5.77 on promo.

8 Blueprint Fino Pale Dry Sherry £7.69

Dependable very dry and very pale aperitif sherry with pungent-tangy aroma and apple-crisp white fruit with the signature yeasty character imparted by the flor that settles atop the wine in cask; 15% alcohol. Serve at white-wine temperature straight from the fridge and don't keep it longer than a few days once opened.

10 No 1 Torre del Oro Palo Cortado Sherry £11.99

The legend 'In Partnership with Lustau' is talismanic on this new addition to the Waitrose & Partners own-label range. One of four Lustau No 1's in the range, it's a cracker, beautifully conker coloured and empyreumatic (pleasingly burnt) on the nose and pungently roasty-figgy-nutty-tangy on the palate; complex, layered, rare classic sherry to serve straight from the fridge or after dinner with cheese as an alternative to port; 19% alcohol.

Enjoying it

Drink or keep?

Wines from supermarkets should be ready to drink as soon as you get them home. Expensive reds of recent vintage, for example from Bordeaux or the Rhône, sold as seasonal specials, might benefit from a few years' 'cellaring'. If in doubt, look up your purchase on a web vintage chart to check.

Some wines certainly need drinking sooner than others. Dry whites and rosés won't improve with time. Good-quality red wines will happily endure, even improve, for years if they're kept at a constant moderate temperature, preferably away from bright light, and on their sides so corks don't dry out. Supermarkets like to advise us on back labels of red wines to consume the product within a year or two. Pay no attention.

Champagne, including supermarket own-label brands, almost invariably improves with keeping. Evolving at rest is what champagne is all about. Continue the process at home. I like to wait for price promotions, buy in bulk and hoard the booty in smug certainty of a bargain that's also an improving asset. None of this applies to any other kind of sparkling wine – especially prosecco.

Of more immediate urgency is the matter of keeping wine in good condition once you've opened it. Recorked leftovers should last a day, but after that the wine will oxidise, turning stale and sour. There is a variety of wine-saving stopper devices, but I have yet to find one that works. My preferred method is to decant leftovers into a smaller bottle with a pull-cork or screwcap. Top it right up.

Early opening

Is there any point in uncorking a wine in advance to allow it to 'breathe'? Absolutely none. The stale air trapped between the top of the wine and the bottom of the cork (or screwcap) disperses at once and the 1cm circle of liquid exposed will have a negligible response to the atmosphere. Decanting the wine will certainly make a difference, but whether it's a beneficial difference is a matter for conjecture – unless you're decanting to get the wine off its lees or sediment.

Beware trying to warm up an icy bottle of red. If you put it close to a heat source, take the cork out first. As the wine warms, even mildly, it gives off gas that will spoil the flavour if it cannot escape.

Chill factor

White wine, rosé and sparkling wines all need to be cold. It's the law. The degree of chill is a personal choice but icy temperatures can mask the flavours of good wines. Bad wines, on the other hand, might benefit from overchilling. The anaesthetic effect removes the sense of taste.

Red wines can respond well to mild chilling. Beaujolais and stalky reds of the Loire such as Chinon and Saumur are brighter when cool, as is Bardolino from Verona and lighter Pinot Noir from everywhere.

Is it off?

Once there was a plague of 'corked' wine. It's over. Wine bottlers have eliminated most of the causes. Principal among them was TCA or trichloroanisole 123, an infection of the raw material from which corks are made, namely the bark of cork oak trees. New technology developed by firms such as Portuguese cork giant Amorim has finally made all cork taint-free.

TCA spawned an alternative-closure industry that has prospered mightily through the supply of polymer stoppers and screwcaps. The polymer products, although unnecessary now that corks are so reliable, persist. They're pointless: awkward to extract and to reinsert, and allegedly less environmentally friendly than natural corks.

Screwcaps persist too, but they have their merits. They obviate the corkscrew and can be replaced on the bottle. They are recyclable. Keep them on the bottles you take to the bottle bank.

Some closures will, of course, occasionally fail due to material faults or malfunctions in bottling that allow air into the bottle. The dull, sour effects on wine of oxidation are obvious, and you should return any offending bottle to the supplier for a replacement or refund. Supermarkets in my experience are pretty good about this.

Wines that are bad because they are poorly made are a bit more complicated. You might just hate it because it's not to your taste – too sweet or too dry, too dense or too light – in which case, bad luck. But if it has classic (though now rare) faults such as mustiness, a vinegar taint (volatile acidity or acetate), cloudiness or a suspension of particles, don't drink it. Recork it and take it back to the supplier.

Glass action

There is something like a consensus in the wine world about the right kind of drinking glass. It should consist of a clear, tulip-shaped bowl on a comfortably long stem. You hold the glass by the stem so you can admire the colour of the wine and keep the bowl free of fingermarks. The bowl is big enough to hold a sensible quantity of wine at about half full. Good wine glasses have a fine bevelled surface at the rim of the bowl. Cheap glasses have a rolled rim that catches your lip and, I believe, materially diminishes the enjoyment of the wine.

Good wine glasses deserve care. Don't put them in the dishwasher. Over time, they'll craze. To maintain the crystal clarity of glasses wash them in hot soapy water, rinse clean with hot water and dry immediately with a glass cloth kept exclusively for this purpose. Sounds a bit nerdy maybe, but it can make all the difference.

What to eat with it?

When tasting a hundred or more wines one after the other and trying to make lucid notes on each of them, the mind can crave diversion. Besides describing the appearance, aroma and taste, as I'm supposed to do, I often muse on what sort of food the wine might suit.

Some of these whimsical observations make it into the finished reports for this book. Like all the rest of it, they are my own subjective opinion, but maybe they help set the wines in some sort of context.

Conventions such as white wine with fish and red with meat might be antiquated, but they can still inhibit choice. If you only like white wine must you abstain on carnivorous occasions – or go veggie? Obviously not. Much better to give detailed thought to the possibilities, and go in for plenty of experimentation.

Ripe whites from grapes such as Chardonnay can match all white meats, cured meats and barbecued meats, and most saucy meat dishes too. With bloody chunks of red meat, exotic whites from the Rhône Valley or Alsace or oaky Rioja Blanco all come immediately to mind.

As for those who prefer red wine at all times, there are few fish dishes that spurn everything red. Maybe a crab salad or a grilled Dover sole. But as soon as you add sauce, red's back on the menu. Again, the answer is to experiment.

Some foods do present particular difficulties. Nibbles such as salty peanuts or vinegary olives will clash with most table wines. So buy some proper dry sherry, chill it down and thrill to the world's best aperitif. Fino, manzanilla and amontillado sherries of real quality now feature in all the best supermarkets – some under own labels.

Eggs are supposed to be inimical to wine. Boiled, fried or poached certainly. But an omelette with a glass of wine, of any colour, is surely a match. Salads, especially those with fruit or tomatoes, get the thumbs-down, but I think it's the dressing. Forgo the vinegar, and salad opens up a vinous vista.

Cheese is a conundrum. Red wine goes with cheese, right? But soft cheeses, particularly goat's, can make red wines taste awfully tinny. You're much better off with an exotic and ripe white wine. Sweet white wines make a famously savoury match with blue cheeses. A better match, I believe, than with their conventional companions, puddings. Hard cheeses such as Cheddar may be fine with some red wines, but even better with a glass of Port.

Wine with curry? Now that incendiary dishes are entirely integrated into the national diet, I suppose this is, uh, a burning question. Big, ripe reds such as Australian Shiraz can stand up to Indian heat, and Argentine Malbec seems appropriate for chilli dishes. Chinese cuisine likes aromatic white wines such as Alsace (or New Zealand) Gewürztraminer, and salsa dishes call for zingy dry whites such as Sauvignon Blanc.

But everyone to their own taste. If there's one universal convention in food and wine matching it must surely be to suit yourself.

A Wine Vocabulary

A brief guide to the use of language across the wine world – on labels, in literature and among the listings in this book

A

AC – *See* Appellation d'Origine Contrôlée.

acidity – Natural acids in grape juice are harnessed by the winemaker to produce clean, crisp flavours. Excess acidity creates rawness or greenness; shortage is indicated by wateriness.

aftertaste – The flavour that lingers in the mouth after swallowing or spitting the wine.

Aglianico – Black grape variety of southern Italy. Vines originally planted by ancient Greek settlers from 600BC in the arid volcanic landscapes of Basilicata and Cilento produce distinctive dark and earthy reds.

Agriculture biologique – On French wine labels, an indication that the wine has been made by organic methods.

Albariño – White grape variety of Spain that makes intriguingly perfumed fresh and tangy dry wines, especially in esteemed Atlantic-facing Rias Baixas region.

alcohol – The alcohol levels in wines are expressed in terms of alcohol by volume ('abv'), that is, the percentage of the volume of the wine that is common, or ethyl, alcohol. A typical wine at 12 per cent abv is thus 12 parts alcohol and, in effect, 88 parts fruit juice. Alcohol is viewed by some health professionals as a poison, but there is actuarial evidence that total abstainers live shorter lives than moderate consumers. The UK Department of Health declares there is no safe level of alcohol consumption, and advises that drinkers should not exceed a weekly number of 'units' of alcohol. A unit is 10ml of pure alcohol, the quantity contained in about half a 175ml glass of wine with 12 per cent alcohol. From 1995, the advisory limit on weekly units was 28 for men and 21 for women. This was reduced in 2016 to 14 for men and women alike.

Alentejo – Wine region of southern Portugal (immediately north of the Algarve), with a fast-improving reputation, especially for sappy, keen reds from local grape varieties including Aragones, Castelão and Trincadeira.

Almansa – DO winemaking region of Spain inland from Alicante, making inexpensive red wines.

Alsace – France's easternmost wine-producing region lies between the Vosges Mountains and the River Rhine, with Germany beyond. These conditions make for the production of some of the world's most delicious and fascinating white wines, always sold under the name of their constituent grapes. Pinot Blanc is the most affordable – and is well worth looking out for. The 'noble' grape varieties of the region are Gewürztraminer, Muscat, Riesling and Pinot Gris and they are always made on a single-variety basis. The richest, most exotic wines are those from individual *grand cru* vineyards, which are named on the label. Some *vendange tardive* (late harvest) wines are made, and tend to be expensive. All the wines are sold in tall, slim green bottles known as flûtes that closely resemble those of the Mosel. The names of producers as well as grape varieties are often German too, so it is widely assumed that Alsace wines are German in style, if not in nationality. But this is not the case in either particular. Alsace wines are dry and quite unique in character – and definitely French.

amarone – Style of red wine made in Valpolicella, Italy. Specially selected grapes are held back from the harvest and stored for several months to dry them out. They are then pressed and fermented into a highly concentrated speciality dry wine. Amarone means 'bitter', describing the dry style of the flavour.

amontillado – *See* sherry.

aperitif – If a wine is thus described, I believe it will give as much pleasure before a meal as with one. Crisp, low-alcohol German wines and other delicately flavoured whites (including many dry Italians) are examples.

appassimento – Italian technique of drying out new-picked grapes to concentrate the sugars. Varying proportions of appassimento fruit are added to the fermentation of speciality wines such as amarone and ripasso.

Appellation d'Origine Contrôlée – Commonly abbreviated to AC or AOC, this is the system under which top-quality wines have been defined in France since 1935. About a third of the country's vast annual output qualifies across about 500 AC (or AOP – see Appellation d'Origine Protégée) zones. The declaration of an AC on the label signifies that the wine meets standards concerning location of vineyards and wineries, grape varieties and limits on harvest per hectare, methods of cultivation and vinification, and alcohol content. Wines are inspected and tasted by state-appointed committees.

Appellation d'Origine Protégée (AOP) – Under European Union rule changes, the AOC system is gradually transforming into AOP. In effect, it means little more than the exchange of 'controlled' with 'protected' on labels. One quirk of the rules is that makers of AOP wines will be able to name the constituent grape variety or varieties on their labels, if they so wish.

Apulia – Anglicised name for Puglia, Italy.

Aragones – Synonym in Portugal, especially in the Alentejo region, for the Tempranillo grape variety of Spain.

Ardèche – Region of southern France to the west of the Rhône river, home to a good IGP zone including the Coteaux de l'Ardèche. Decent-value reds from Syrah and Cabernet Sauvignon grapes, and less interesting dry whites.

Arneis – White grape variety of Piedmont, north-west Italy. Makes dry whites with a certain almondy richness at often-inflated prices.

Assyrtiko – White grape variety of Greece now commonly named on dry white wines, sometimes of great quality, from the mainland and islands.

Asti – Town and major winemaking centre in Piedmont, Italy. The sparkling (spumante) wines made from Moscato grapes are inexpensive and sweet with a modest 5 to 7 per cent alcohol. Vivid red wine Barbera d'Asti also produced.

attack – In wine-tasting, the first impression made by the wine in the mouth.

Auslese – German wine-quality designation. *See* QmP.

B

Baga – Black grape variety indigenous to Portugal. Makes famously concentrated, juicy reds of deep colour from the grapes' particularly thick skins. Look out for this name, now quite frequently quoted as the varietal on Portuguese wine labels.

balance – A big word in the vocabulary of wine tasting. Respectable wine must get two key things right: lots of fruitiness from the sweet grape juice, and plenty of acidity so the sweetness is 'balanced' with the crispness familiar in good dry whites and the dryness that marks out good reds. Some wines are noticeably 'well balanced' in that they have memorable fruitiness and the clean, satisfying 'finish' (last flavour in the mouth) that ideal acidity imparts.

Barbera – Black grape variety originally of Piedmont in Italy. Most commonly seen as Barbera d'Asti, the vigorously fruity red wine made around Asti – once better known for sweet sparkling Asti Spumante. Barbera grapes are now cultivated in South America, producing less-interesting wine than at home in Italy.

Bardolino – Once fashionable, light red wine DOC of Veneto, north-west Italy. Bardolino is made principally from Corvina Veronese grapes plus Rondinella, Molinara and Negrara. Best wines are supposed to be those labelled Bardolino Superiore, a DOCG created in 2002. This classification closely specifies the permissible grape varieties and sets the alcohol level at a minimum of 12 per cent.

Barossa Valley – Famed vineyard region north of Adelaide, Australia, produces hearty reds principally from Shiraz, Cabernet Sauvignon and Grenache grapes, plus plenty of lush white wine from Chardonnay. Also known for limey, long-lived, mineral dry whites from Riesling grapes.

barrique – Barrel in French. *En barrique* on a wine label signifies the wine has been matured in casks rather than tanks.

Beaujolais – Unique red wines from the southern reaches of Burgundy, France, are made from Gamay grapes. Beaujolais nouveau, now unfashionable, provides a friendly introduction to the bouncy, red-fruit style of the wine, but for the authentic experience, go for Beaujolais Villages, from the region's better, northern vineyards. There are ten AC zones within this northern sector making wines under their own names. Known as the *crus*, these are Brouilly, Chénas, Chiroubles, Côte de Brouilly, Fleurie, Juliénas, Morgon, Moulin à Vent, Regnié and St Amour. Prices are higher than those for Beaujolais Villages, but not always justifiably so.

Beaumes de Venise – Village near Châteauneuf du Pape in France's Rhône valley, famous for sweet and alcoholic wine from Muscat grapes. Delicious, grapey wines. A small number of growers also make strong (sometimes rather tough) red wines under the village name.

Beaune – One of the two centres (the other is Nuits St Georges) of the Côte d'Or, the winemaking heart of Burgundy in France. Three of the region's humbler appellations take the name of the town: Côtes de Beaune, Côtes de Beaune Villages and Hautes Côtes de Beaune.

berry fruit – Some red wines deliver a burst of flavour in the mouth that corresponds to biting into a newly picked berry – strawberry, blackberry, etc. So a wine described as having berry fruit (by this writer, anyway) has freshness, liveliness and immediate appeal.

bianco – White wine, Italy.

Bical – White grape variety principally of Dão region of northern Portugal. Not usually identified on labels, because most of it goes into inexpensive sparkling wines. Can make still wines of very refreshing crispness.

biodynamics – A cultivation method taking the organic approach several steps further. Biodynamic winemakers plant and tend their vineyards according to a date and time calendar 'in harmony' with the movements of the planets. Some of France's best-known wine estates subscribe, and many more are going that way. It might all sound bonkers, but it's salutary to learn that biodynamics is based on principles first described by the eminent Austrian educationist Rudolph Steiner.

bite – In wine-tasting, the impression on the palate of a wine with plenty of acidity and, often, tannin.

blanc – White wine, France.

blanc de blancs – White wine from white grapes, France. May seem to be stating the obvious, but some white wines (e.g. champagne) are made, partially or entirely, from black grapes.

blanc de noirs – White wine from black grapes, France. Usually sparkling (especially champagne) made from black Pinot Meunier and Pinot Noir grapes, with no Chardonnay or other white varieties.

blanco – White wine, Spain and Portugal.

Blauer Zweigelt – Black grape variety of Austria, making a large proportion of the country's red wines, some of excellent quality.

Bobal – Black grape variety mostly of south-eastern Spain. Thick skin is good for colour and juice contributes acidity to blends.

bodega – In Spain, a wine producer or wine shop.

Bonarda – Black grape variety of northern Italy. Now more widely planted in Argentina, where it makes some well-regarded red wines.

botrytis – Full name, *botrytis cinerea*, is that of a beneficent fungus that can attack ripe grape bunches late in the season, shrivelling the berries to a gruesome-looking mess, which yields concentrated juice of prized sweetness. Cheerfully known as 'noble rot', this fungus is actively encouraged by winemakers in regions as diverse as Sauternes (in Bordeaux), Monbazillac (in Bergerac), the Rhine and Mosel valleys, Hungary's Tokaji region and South Australia to make ambrosial dessert wines.

bouncy – The feel in the mouth of a red wine with young, juicy fruitiness. Good Beaujolais is bouncy, as are many north-west-Italian wines from Barbera and Dolcetto grapes.

Bourgogne Grand Ordinaire – Former AC of Burgundy, France. *See* Coteaux Bourguignons.

Bourgueil – Appellation of Loire Valley, France. Long-lived red wines from Cabernet Franc grapes.

briary – In wine tasting, associated with the flavours of fruit from prickly bushes such as blackberries.

brûlé – Pleasant burnt-toffee taste or smell, as in crème brûlée.

brut – Driest style of sparkling wine. Originally French, for very dry champagnes specially developed for the British market, but now used for sparkling wines from all round the world.

Buzet – Little-seen AC of south-west France overshadowed by Bordeaux but producing some characterful ripe reds.

C

Cabardès – AC for red and rosé wines from area north of Carcassonne, Aude, France. Principally Cabernet Sauvignon and Merlot grapes.

Cabernet Franc – Black grape variety originally of France. It makes the light-bodied and keenly edged red wines of the Loire Valley – such as Chinon and Saumur. And it is much grown in Bordeaux, especially in the appellation of St Emilion. Also now planted in Argentina, Australia and North America. Wines, especially in the Loire, are characterised by a leafy, sappy style and bold fruitiness. Most are best enjoyed young.

Cabernet Sauvignon – Black (or, rather, blue) grape variety now grown in virtually every wine-producing nation. When perfectly ripened, the grapes are smaller than many other varieties and have particularly thick skins.

This means that when pressed, Cabernet grapes have a high proportion of skin to juice – and that makes for wine with lots of colour and tannin. In Bordeaux, the grape's traditional home, the grandest Cabernet-based wines have always been known as *vins de garde* (wines to keep) because they take years, even decades, to evolve as the effect of all that skin extraction preserves the fruit all the way to magnificent maturity. But in today's impatient world, these grapes are exploited in modern winemaking techniques to produce the sublime flavours of mature Cabernet without having to hang around for lengthy periods awaiting maturation. While there's nothing like a fine, ten-year-old claret (and few quite as expensive), there are many excellent Cabernets from around the world that amply illustrate this grape's characteristics. Classic smells and flavours include blackcurrants, cedar wood, chocolate, tobacco – even violets.

Cahors – An AC of the Lot Valley in south-west France once famous for 'black wine'. This was a curious concoction of straightforward wine mixed with a soupy must, made by boiling up new-pressed juice to concentrate it (through evaporation) before fermentation. The myth is still perpetuated that Cahors wine continues to be made in this way, but production on this basis actually ceased 150 years ago. Cahors today is no stronger, or blacker, than the wines of neighbouring appellations. Principal grape variety is Malbec, known locally as Cot.

Cairanne – Village of the appellation collectively known as the Côtes du Rhône in southern France. Cairanne is one of several villages entitled to put their name on the labels of wines made within their AC boundary, and the appearance of this name is quite reliably an indicator of quality.

Calatayud – DO (quality wine zone) near Zaragoza in the Aragon region of northern Spain where they're making some astonishingly good wines at bargain prices, mainly reds from Garnacha and Tempranillo grapes. These are the varieties that go into the polished and oaky wines of Rioja, but in Calatayud, the wines are dark, dense and decidedly different.

Cannonau – Black grape native to Sardinia by name, but in fact the same variety as the ubiquitous Grenache of France (and Garnacha of Spain).

cantina sociale – *See* co-op.

Carignan – Black grape variety of Mediterranean France. It is rarely identified on labels, but is a major constituent of wines from the southern Rhône and Languedoc-Roussillon regions. Known as Carignano in Italy and Cariñena in Spain.

Cariñena – A region of north-east Spain, south of Navarra, known for substantial reds, as well as the Spanish name for the Carignan grape (*qv*).

Carmenère – Black grape variety once widely grown in Bordeaux but abandoned due to cultivation problems. Lately revived in South America where it is producing fine wines, sometimes with echoes of Bordeaux.

cassis – As a tasting note, signifies a wine that has a noticeable blackcurrant-concentrate flavour or smell. Much associated with the Cabernet Sauvignon grape.

Castelao – Portuguese black grape variety. Same as Periquita.

Catarratto – White grape variety of Sicily. In skilled hands it can make anything from keen, green-fruit dry whites to lush, oaked super-ripe styles. Also used for Marsala.

cat's pee – In tasting notes, a jocular reference to the smell of a certain style of Sauvignon Blanc wine.

cava – The sparkling wine of Spain. Most originates in Catalonia, but the Denominación de Origen (DO) guarantee of authenticity is open to producers in many regions of the country. Much cava is very reasonably priced even though it is made by the same method as champagne – second fermentation in bottle, known in Spain as the *método clásico.*

CdR – Côtes du Rhône. My own shorthand.

cépage – Grape variety, French. 'Cépage Merlot' on a label simply means the wine is made largely or exclusively from Merlot grapes.

Chablis – Northernmost AC of France's Burgundy region. Its dry white wines from Chardonnay grapes are known for their fresh and steely style, but the best wines also age very gracefully into complex classics.

Chambourcin – Sounds like a cream cheese but it's a relatively modern (1963) French hybrid black grape that makes some good non-appellation lightweight-but-concentrated reds in the Loire Valley and now some heftier versions in Australia.

champagne – The sparkling wine of the strictly defined Champagne region of France, made by the equally strictly defined champagne method.

Chardonnay – Possibly the world's most popular grape variety. Said to originate from the village of Chardonnay in the Mâconnais region of southern Burgundy, the vine is now planted in every wine-producing nation. Wines are commonly characterised by generous colour and sweet-apple smell, but styles range from lean and sharp to opulently rich. Australia started the craze for oaked Chardonnay, the gold-coloured, super-ripe, buttery 'upfront' wines that are a caricature of lavish and outrageously expensive burgundies such as Meursault and Puligny-Montrachet. Rich to the point of egginess, these Aussie pretenders are now giving way to a sleeker, more minerally style with much less oak presence – if any at all. California and Chile, New Zealand and South Africa are competing hard to imitate the Burgundian style, and Australia's success in doing so.

Châteauneuf du Pape – Famed appellation centred on a picturesque village of the southern Rhône valley in France where in the 1320s French Pope Clement V had a splendid new château built for himself as a summer retreat amidst his vineyards. The red wines of the AC, which can be made from 13 different grape varieties but principally Grenache, Syrah and Mourvèdre, are regarded as the best of the southern Rhône and have become rather expensive – but they can be sensationally good. Expensive white wines are also made.

Chenin Blanc – White grape variety of the Loire Valley, France. Now also grown farther afield, especially in South Africa. Makes dry, soft white wines and also rich, sweet styles.

cherry – In wine tasting, either a pale red colour or, more commonly, a smell or flavour akin to the sun-warmed, bursting sweet ripeness of cherries. Many Italian wines, from lightweights such as Bardolino and Valpolicella to serious Chianti, have this character. 'Black cherry' as a description is often used of Merlot wines – meaning they are sweet but have a firmness of mouthfeel associated with the thicker skins of black cherries.

Cinsault – Black grape variety of southern France, where it is invariably blended with others in wines of all qualities from country reds to pricy appellations such as Châteauneuf du Pape. Also much planted in South Africa. The effect in wine is to add keen aromas (sometimes compared with turpentine) and softness to the blend. The name is often spelt Cinsaut.

Clape, La – A small *cru* (defined quality-vineyard area) within the Coteaux du Languedoc where the growers make some seriously delicious red wines, mainly from Carignan, Grenache and Syrah grapes. A name worth looking out for on labels from the region.

claret – The red wine of Bordeaux, France. Old British nickname from Latin *clarus*, meaning 'clear', recalling a time when the red wines of the region were much lighter in colour than they are now.

clarete – On Spanish labels indicates a pale-coloured red wine. Tinto signifies a deeper hue.

classed growth – English translation of French *cru classé* describes a group of 60 individual wine estates in the Médoc district of Bordeaux, which in 1855 were granted this new status on the basis that their wines were the most expensive of the day. The classification was a promotional wheeze to attract attention to the Bordeaux stand at that year's Great Exhibition in Paris. Amazingly, all of the wines concerned are still in production and most still occupy more or less their original places in the pecking order price-wise. The league was divided up into five divisions from *Premier Grand Cru Classé* (just four wines originally, with one promoted in 1971 – the only change ever made to the classification) to *Cinquième Grand Cru Classé*. Other regions of Bordeaux, notably Graves and St Emilion, have since imitated Médoc and introduced their own rankings of *cru classé* estates.

classic – An overused term in every respect – wine descriptions being no exception. In this book, the word is used to describe a very good wine of its type. So, a 'classic' Cabernet Sauvignon is one that is recognisably and admirably characteristic of that grape.

Classico – Under Italy's wine laws, this word appended to the name of a DOC or DOCG zone has an important significance. The classico wines of the region can only be made from vineyards lying in the best-rated areas, and wines thus labelled (e.g. Chianti Classico, Soave Classico, Valpolicella Classico) can be reliably counted on to be a cut above the rest.

Colombard – White grape variety of southern France. Once employed almost entirely for making the wine that is distilled for armagnac and cognac brandies, but lately restored to varietal prominence in the Côtes de Gascogne where high-tech wineries turn it into a fresh and crisp, if unchallenging, dry wine at a budget price. But beware, cheap Colombard (especially from South Africa) can still be very dull.

Conca de Barbera – Winemaking region of Catalonia, Spain.

co-op – Very many of France's good-quality, inexpensive wines are made by co-operatives. These are wine-producing centres whose members, and joint-owners, are local *vignerons* (vine growers). Each year they sell their harvests to the co-op for turning into branded wines. In Italy, co-op wines can be identified by the words *Cantina Sociale* on the label and in Germany by the term *Winzergenossenschaft.*

Corbières – A name to look out for. It's an AC of France's Midi (deep south) and produces countless robust reds and a few interesting whites, often at bargain prices.

Cortese – White grape variety of Piedmont, Italy. At its best, makes delicious, keenly brisk and fascinating wines, including those of the Gavi DOCG. Worth seeking out.

Costières de Nîmes – Until 1989, this AC of southern France was known as the Costières de Gard. It forms a buffer between the southern Rhône and Languedoc-Roussillon regions, and makes wines from broadly the same range of grape varieties. It's a name to look out for, the best red wines being notable for their concentration of colour and fruit, with the earthy-spiciness of the better Rhône wines and a likeable liquorice note. A few good white wines, too, and even a decent rosé or two.

Côte – In French, it simply means a side, or slope, of a hill. The implication in wine terms is that the grapes come from a vineyard ideally situated for maximum sunlight, good drainage and the unique soil conditions prevailing on the hill in question. It's fair enough to claim that vines grown on slopes might get more sunlight than those grown on the flat, but there is no guarantee whatsoever that any wine labelled 'Côtes du' this or that is made from grapes grown on a hillside anyway. Côtes du Rhône wines are a case in point. Many 'Côtes' wines come from entirely level vineyards and it is worth remembering that many of the vineyards of Bordeaux, producing most of the world's priciest wines, are little short of prairie-flat. The quality factor is determined much more significantly by the weather and the talents of the winemaker.

Coteaux Bourguignons – Generic AC of Burgundy, France, since 2011 for red and rosé wines from Pinot Noir and Gamay grapes, and white wines from (principally) Chardonnay and Bourgogne Aligoté grapes. The AC replaces the former appellation Bourgogne Grand Ordinaire.

Côtes de Blaye – Appellation Contrôlée zone of Bordeaux on the right bank of the River Gironde, opposite the more prestigious Médoc zone of the left bank. Best-rated vineyards qualify for the AC Premières Côtes de Blaye. A couple of centuries ago, Blaye (pronounced 'bligh') was the grander of the two, and even today makes some wines that compete well for quality, and at a fraction of the price of wines from its more fashionable rival across the water.

Côtes de Bourg – AC neighbouring Côtes de Blaye, making red wines of decent quality and value.

Côtes du Luberon – Appellation Contrôlée zone of Provence in south-east France. Wines, mostly red, are similar in style to Côtes du Rhône.

Côtes du Rhône – One of the biggest and best-known appellations of south-east France, covering an area roughly defined by the southern reaches of the valley of the River Rhône. The Côtes du Rhône AC achieves notably consistent quality at all points along the price scale. Lots of brilliant-value warm and spicy reds, principally from Grenache and Syrah grapes. There are also some white and rosé wines.

Côtes du Rhône Villages – Appellation within the larger Côtes du Rhône AC for wine of supposed superiority made in a number of zones associated with a long list of nominated individual villages.

Côtes du Roussillon – Huge appellation of south-west France known for strong, dark, peppery reds often offering very decent value.

Côtes du Roussillon Villages – Appellation for superior wines from a number of nominated locations within the larger Roussillon AC. Some of these village wines can be of exceptional quality and value.

crianza – Means 'nursery' in Spanish. On Rioja and Navarra wines, the designation signifies a wine that has been nursed through a maturing period of at least a year in oak casks and a further six months in bottle before being released for sale.

cru – A word that crops up with confusing regularity on French wine labels. It means 'the growing' or 'the making' of a wine and asserts that the wine concerned is from a specific vineyard. Under the Appellation Contrôlée rules, countless *crus* are classified in various hierarchical ranks. Hundreds of individual vineyards are described as *premier cru* or *grand cru* in the classic wine regions of Alsace, Bordeaux, Burgundy and Champagne. The common denominator is that the wine can be counted on to be expensive. On humbler wines, the use of the word *cru* tends to be mere decoration.

cru classé – *See* classed growth.

cuve – A vat for wine. French.

cuvée – French for the wine in a *cuve*, or vat. The word is much used on labels to imply that the wine is from just one vat, and thus of unique, unblended character. *Première cuvée* is supposedly the best wine from a given pressing because it comes from the free-run juice of grapes crushed by their own weight before pressing begins. Subsequent *cuvées* will have been from harsher pressings, grinding the grape pulp to extract the last drops of juice.

D

Dão – Major wine-producing region of northern Portugal now turning out much more interesting reds than it used to – worth looking out for anything made by mega-producer Sogrape.

demi sec – 'Half-dry' style of French (and some other) wines. Beware. It can mean anything from off-dry to cloyingly sweet.

DO – Denominación de Origen, Spain's wine-regulating scheme, similar to France's AC, but older – the first DO region was Rioja, from 1926. DO wines are Spain's best, accounting for a third of the nation's annual production.

DOC – Stands for Denominazione di Origine Controllata, Italy's equivalent of France's AC. The wines are made according to the stipulations of each of the system's 300-plus denominated zones of origin, along with a further 74 zones, which enjoy the superior classification of DOCG (DOC with *e Garantita* – guaranteed – appended).

DOCa – *Denominación de Origen Calificada* is Spain's highest regional wine classification; currently only Priorat and Rioja qualify.

DOP – Denominazione di Origine Protetta is an alternative classification to DOC (*qv*) under EU directive in Italy, comparable to AOP (*qv*) in France, but not yet widely adopted.

Durif – Rare black grape variety mostly of California, where it is also known as Petite Sirah, with some plantings in Australia.

E

earthy – A tricky word in the wine vocabulary. In this book, its use is meant to be complimentary. It indicates that the wine somehow suggests the soil the grapes were grown in, even (perhaps a shade too poetically) the landscape in which the vineyards lie. The amazing-value red wines of the torrid, volcanic southernmost regions of Italy are often described as earthy. This is an association with the pleasantly 'scorched' back-flavour in wines made from the ultra-ripe harvests of this near-sub-tropical part of the world.

edge – A wine with edge is one with evident (although not excessive) acidity.

élevé – 'Brought up' in French. Much used on wine labels where the wine has been matured (brought up) in oak barrels, *élevé en fûts de chêne*, to give it extra dimensions.

Entre Deux Mers – Meaning 'between two seas', it's a region lying between the Dordogne and Garonne rivers of Bordeaux, now mainly known for dry white wines from Sauvignon Blanc and Semillon grapes.

Estremadura – Wine-producing region occupying Portugal's coastal area north of Lisbon. Lots of interesting wines from indigenous grape varieties, often at bargain prices. If a label mentions Estremadura, it is a safe rule that there might be something good within.

Extremadura – Minor wine-producing region of western Spain abutting the frontier with Portugal's Alentejo region. Not to be confused with Estremadura of Portugal (above).

F

Falanghina – Revived ancient grape variety of southern Italy now making some superbly fresh and tangy white wines.

Faugères – AC of the Languedoc in south-west France. Source of many hearty, economic reds.

Feteasca – White grape variety widely grown in Romania. Name means 'maiden's grape' and the wine tends to be soft and slightly sweet.

Fiano – White grape variety of the Campania of southern Italy and Sicily, lately revived. It is said to have been cultivated by the ancient Romans for a wine called Apianum.

finish – The last flavour lingering in the mouth after wine has been swallowed.

fino – Pale and very dry style of sherry. You drink it thoroughly chilled – and you don't keep it any longer after opening than other dry white wines. Needs to be fresh to be at its best.

Fitou – AC of Languedoc, France. Red wines principally from Carignan, Grenache, Mourvèdre and Syrah grapes.

flabby – Fun word describing a wine that tastes dilute or watery, with insufficient acidity.

Frappato – Black grape variety of Sicily. Light red wines.

fruit – In tasting terms, the fruit is the greater part of the overall flavour of a wine. The wine is, after all, composed entirely of fruit

G

Gamay – The black grape that makes all red Beaujolais and some ordinary burgundy. It is a pretty safe rule to avoid Gamay wines from other regions.

Garganega – White grape variety of the Veneto region of north-east Italy. Best known as the principal ingredient of Soave, but occasionally included in varietal blends and mentioned as such on labels. Correctly pronounced 'gar-GAN-iga'.

Garnacha – Spanish black grape variety synonymous with Grenache of France. It is blended with Tempranillo to make the red wines of Rioja and Navarra, and is now quite widely cultivated elsewhere in Spain to make grippingly fruity varietals.

garrigue – Arid land of France's deep south giving its name to a style of red wine that notionally evokes the herby, heated, peppery flavours associated with such a landscape and its flora. A tricky metaphor.

Gavi – DOCG for dry aromatic white wine from Cortese grapes in Piedmont, north-west Italy. Trendy Gavi di Gavi wines tend to be enjoyably lush, but are rather expensive.

Gewürztraminer – One of the great grape varieties of Alsace, France. At their best, the wines are perfumed with lychees and are richly, spicily fruity, yet quite dry. Gewürztraminer from Alsace can be expensive, but the grape is also grown with some success in Germany, Italy, New Zealand and South America, at more approachable prices. Pronounced 'ge-VOORTS-traminner'.

Givry – AC for red and white wines in the Côte Chalonnaise sub-region of Burgundy. Source of some wonderfully natural-tasting reds that might be lighter than those of the more prestigious Côte d'Or to the north, but have great merits of their own. Relatively, the wines are often underpriced.

Glera – New official name for the Prosecco grape of northern Italy.

Godello – White grape variety of Galicia, Spain.

Graciano – Black grape variety of Spain that is one of the minor constituents of Rioja. Better known in its own right in Australia where it can make dense, spicy, long-lived red wines.

green – I don't often use this in the pejorative. Green, to me, is a likeable degree of freshness, especially in Sauvignon Blanc wines.

Grecanico – White grape variety of southern Italy, especially Sicily. Aromatic, grassy dry white wines.

Greco – White grape variety of southern Italy believed to be of ancient Greek origin. Big-flavoured dry white wines.

Grenache – The mainstay of the wines of the southern Rhône Valley in France. Grenache is usually the greater part of the mix in Côtes du Rhône reds and is widely planted right across the neighbouring Languedoc-Roussillon region. It's a big-cropping variety that thrives even in the hottest climates and is really a blending grape – most commonly with Syrah, the noble variety of the northern Rhône. Few French wines are labelled with its name, but the grape has caught on in Australia in a big way and it is now becoming a familiar varietal, known for strong, dark liquorous reds. Grenache is the French name for what is originally a Spanish variety, Garnacha.

Grillo – White grape of Sicily said to be among the island's oldest indigenous varieties, pre-dating the arrival of the Greeks in 600 BC. Much used for fortified Marsala, it has lately been revived for interesting, aromatic dry table wines.

grip – In wine-tasting terminology, the sensation in the mouth produced by a wine that has a healthy quantity of tannin in it. A wine with grip is a good wine. A wine with too much tannin, or which is still too young (the tannin hasn't 'softened' with age) is not described as having grip, but as mouth-puckering – or simply undrinkable.

Grolleau – Black grape variety of the Loire Valley principally cultivated for Rosé d'Anjou.

Gros Plant – White grape variety of the Pays Nantais in France's Loire estuary; synonymous with the Folle Blanche grape of south-west France.

Grüner Veltliner – The 'national' white-wine grape of Austria. In the past it made mostly soft, German-style everyday wines, but now is behind some excellent dry styles, too.

H

halbtrocken – 'Half-dry' in Germany's wine vocabulary. A reassurance that the wine is not a sugared Liebfraumilch-style confection.

hard – In red wine, a flavour denoting excess tannin, probably due to immaturity.

Haut-Médoc – Extensive AC of Bordeaux accounting for the greater part of the vineyard area to the north of the city of Bordeaux west of the Gironde river. The Haut-Médoc incorporates the prestigious commune-ACs of Listrac, Margaux, Moulis, Pauillac, St Estèphe and St Julien.

Hermitage – AC of northern Rhône Valley, France for red wines from Syrah grapes and some whites. Hermitage is also the regional name in South Africa for the Cinsaut grape.

hock – The wine of Germany's Rhine river valleys. Traditionally, but no longer consistently, it comes in brown bottles, as distinct from the wine of the Mosel river valleys – which comes in green ones.

Hunter Valley – Long-established (1820s) wine-producing region of New South Wales, Australia.

I

Indicación Geográfica Protegida (IGP) – Spain's country-wine quality designation covers 46 zones across the country. Wines made under the IGP can be labelled Vino de la Tierra.

Indication Géographique Protégée (IGP) – Introduced to France in 2010 under EU-wide wine-designation rules, IGP covers the wines previously known as vins de pays. Some wines are currently labelled IGP, but established vins de pays producers are redesignating slowly, if at all, and are not obliged to do so. Some will abbreviate, so, for example, Vin de Pays d'Oc shortens to Pays d'Oc.

Indicazione Geografica Tipica (IGT) – Italian wine-quality designation, broadly equivalent to France's IGP. The label has to state the geographical location of the vineyard and will often (but not always) state the principal grape varieties from which the wine is made.

isinglass – A gelatinous material used in fining (clarifying) wine. It is derived from fish bladders and consequently is eschewed by makers of 'vegetarian' or 'vegan' wines.

J

jammy – The 'sweetness' in dry red wines is supposed to evoke ripeness rather than sugariness. Sometimes, flavours include a sweetness reminiscent of jam. Usually a fault in the winemaking technique.

Jerez – Wine town of Andalucia, Spain, and home to sherry. The English word 'sherry' is a simple mispronunciation of Jerez.

joven – Young wine, Spanish. In regions such as Rioja, *vino joven* is a synonym for *sin crianza*, which means 'without ageing' in cask or bottle.

Jura – Wine region of eastern France incorporating four AOCs, Arbois, Château-Chalon, Côtes du Jura and L'Etoile. Known for still red, white and rosé wines and sparkling wines as well as exotic *vin de paille* and *vin jaune*.

Jurançon – Appellation for white wines from Courbu and Manseng grapes at Pau, south-west France.

K

Kabinett – Under Germany's bewildering wine-quality rules, this is a classification of a top-quality (QmP) wine. Expect a keen, dry, racy style. The name comes from the cabinet or cupboard in which winemakers traditionally kept their most treasured bottles.

Kekfrankos – Black grape variety of Hungary, particularly the Sopron region, which makes some of the country's more interesting red wines, characterised by colour and spiciness. Same variety as Austria's Blaufrankisch.

L

Ladoix – Unfashionable AC at northern edge of Côtes de Beaune makes some of Burgundy's true bargain reds. A name to look out for.

Lambrusco – The name is that of a black grape variety widely grown across northern Italy. True Lambrusco wine is red, dry and very slightly sparkling, and enjoying a current vogue in Britain.

Languedoc-Roussillon – Extensive wine region of southern France incorporating numerous ACs and IGP zones, notably the Pays d'Oc and Côtes de Roussillon.

lees – The detritus of the winemaking process that collects in the bottom of the vat or cask. Wines left for extended periods on the lees can acquire extra dimensions of flavour, in particular a 'leesy' creaminess.

legs – The liquid residue left clinging to the sides of the glass after wine has been swirled. The persistence of the legs is an indicator of the weight of alcohol. Also known as 'tears'.

lieu dit – This is starting to appear on French wine labels. It translates as an 'agreed place' and is an area of vineyard defined as of particular character or merit, but not classified under wine law. Usually, the *lieu dit*'s name is stated, with the implication that the wine in question has special merit.

liquorice – The pungent, slightly burnt flavours of this confection are detectable in some wines made from very ripe grapes, for example, the Malbec harvested in Argentina and several varieties grown in the very hot vineyards of southernmost Italy. A close synonym is 'tarry'. This characteristic is by no means a fault in red wine, unless very dominant, but it can make for a challenging flavour that might not appeal to all tastes.

liquorous – Wines of great weight and glyceriney texture (evidenced by the 'legs', or 'tears', which cling to the glass after the wine has been swirled) are always noteworthy. The connection with liquor is drawn in respect of the feel of the wine in the mouth, rather than with the higher alcoholic strength of spirits.

Lirac – Village and AC of southern Rhône Valley, France. A near-neighbour of the esteemed appellation of Châteauneuf du Pape, Lirac makes red wine of comparable depth and complexity, at competitive prices.

Lugana – DOC of Lombardy, Italy, known for a dry white wine that is often of real distinction – rich, almondy stuff from the ubiquitous Trebbiano grape.

M

Macabeo – One of the main grapes used for cava, the sparkling wine of Spain. It is the same grape as Viura.

Mâcon – Town and collective appellation of southern Burgundy, France. Minerally white wines from Chardonnay grapes and light reds from Pinot Noir and some Gamay. The better ones, and the ones exported, have the AC Mâcon-Villages and there are individual village wines with their own ACs including Mâcon-Clessé, Mâcon-Viré and Mâcon-Lugny.

Malbec – Black grape variety grown on a small scale in Bordeaux, and the mainstay of the wines of Cahors in France's Dordogne region under the name Cot. Now much better known for producing big butch reds in Argentina.

malolactic fermentation – In winemaking, a common natural bacterial action following alcoholic fermentation, converting malic (apple) acid into lactic (milk) acid. The effect is to reduce tartness and to boost creaminess in the wine. Adding lactic bacteria to wine to promote the process is widely practised.

manzanilla – Pale, very dry sherry of Sanlucar de Barrameda, a resort town on the Bay of Cadiz in Spain. Manzanilla is proud to be distinct from the pale, very dry fino sherry of the main producing town of Jerez de la Frontera an hour's drive inland. Drink it chilled and fresh – it goes downhill in an opened bottle after just a few days, even if kept (as it should be) in the fridge.

Margaret River – Vineyard region of Western Australia regarded as ideal for grape varieties including Cabernet Sauvignon. It has a relatively cool climate and a reputation for making sophisticated wines, both red and white.

Marlborough – Best-known vineyard region of New Zealand's South Island has a cool climate and a name for brisk but cerebral Sauvignon Blanc and Chardonnay wines.

Marsanne – White grape variety of the northern Rhône Valley and, increasingly, of the wider south of France. It's known for making well-coloured wines with heady aroma and nuanced fruit.

Mataro – Black grape variety of Australia. It's the same as the Mourvèdre of France and Monastrell of Spain.

Mazuelo – Spanish name for France's black grape variety Carignan.

McLaren Vale – Vineyard region south of Adelaide in south-east Australia. Known for blockbuster Shiraz (and Chardonnay) that can be of great balance and quality from winemakers who manage to keep the ripeness under control.

meaty – In wine-tasting, a weighty, rich red wine style.

Mencia – Black grape variety of Galicia and north-west Spain. Light red wines.

Mendoza – Wine region of Argentina. Lying to the east of the Andes mountains, just about opposite the best vineyards of Chile on the other side, Mendoza accounts for the bulk of Argentine wine production.

Merlot – One of the great black wine grapes of Bordeaux, and now grown all over the world. The name is said to derive from the French *merle*, a blackbird. Characteristics of Merlot-based wines attract descriptions such as 'plummy' and 'plump' with black-cherry aromas. The grapes are larger than most, and thus have less skin in proportion to their flesh. This means the resulting wines have less tannin than wines from smaller-berry varieties such as Cabernet Sauvignon, and are therefore, in the Bordeaux context at least, more suitable for drinking while still relatively young.

middle palate – In wine-tasting, the impression given by the wine after the first impact on 'entry' and before the 'finish' when the wine is swallowed.

Midi – Catch-all term for the deep south of France west of the Rhône Valley.

mineral – Irresistible term in wine-tasting. To me it evokes flavours such as the stone-pure freshness of some Loire dry whites, or the flinty quality of the more austere style of the Chardonnay grape, especially in Chablis. Mineral really just means something mined, as in dug out of the ground, like iron ore (as in 'steely' whites) or rock, as in, er, stone. Maybe there's something in it, but I am not entirely confident.

Minervois – AC for (mostly) red wines from vineyards around the Roman-founded town of Minerve in the Languedoc-Roussillon region of France. Often good value. The recently elevated Minervois La Livinière AC is a sort of Minervois *grand cru.*

Monastrell – Black grape variety of Spain, widely planted in Mediterranean regions for inexpensive wines notable for their high alcohol and toughness – though they can mature into excellent, soft reds. The variety is known in France as Mourvèdre and in Australia as Mataro.

Monbazillac – AC for sweet, dessert wines within the wider appellation of Bergerac in south-west France. Made from the same grape varieties (principally Sauvignon and Semillon) that go into the much costlier counterpart wines of Barsac and Sauternes near Bordeaux, these stickies from botrytis-affected, late-harvested grapes can be delicious and good value for money.

Montalcino – Hill town of Tuscany, Italy, and a DOCG for strong and very long-lived red wines from Brunello grapes. The wines are mostly very expensive. Rosso di Montalcino, a DOC for the humbler wines of the zone, is often a good buy.

Montepulciano – Black grape variety of Italy. Best known in Montepulciano d'Abruzzo, the juicy, purply-black and bramble-fruited red of the Abruzzi region midway down Italy's Adriatic side. Also the grape in the rightly popular hearty reds of Rosso Conero from around Ancona in the Marches. Not to be confused with the hill town of Montepulciano in Tuscany, famous for expensive Vino Nobile di Montepulciano wine, made from Sangiovese grapes.

morello – Lots of red wines have smells and flavours redolent of cherries. Morello cherries, among the darkest coloured and sweetest of all varieties and the preferred choice of cherry-brandy producers, have a distinct sweetness resembled by some wines made from Merlot grapes. A morello whiff or taste is generally very welcome.

Moscatel – Spanish Muscat.

Moscato – *See* Muscat.

moselle – The wine of Germany's Mosel river valleys, collectively known for winemaking purposes as the Mosel-Saar-Ruwer. The wine always comes in slim, green bottles, as distinct from the brown bottles traditionally, but no longer exclusively, employed for Rhine wines.

Mourvèdre – Widely planted black grape variety of southern France. It's an ingredient in many of the wines of Provence, the Rhône and Languedoc, including the ubiquitous Pays d'Oc. It's a hot-climate vine and the wine is usually blended with other varieties to give sweet aromas and 'backbone' to the mix. Known as Mataro in Australia and Monastrell in Spain.

Muscadet – One of France's most familiar everyday whites, made from a grape called the Melon or Melon de Bourgogne. It comes from vineyards at the estuarial end of the River Loire, and has a sea-breezy freshness about it. The better wines are reckoned to be those from the vineyards in the Sèvre et Maine region, and many are made *sur lie* – 'on the lees' – meaning that the wine is left in contact with the yeasty deposit of its fermentation until just before bottling, in an endeavour to add interest to what can sometimes be an acidic and fruitless style.

Muscat – Grape variety with origins in ancient Greece, and still grown widely among the Aegean islands for the production of sweet white wines. Muscats are the wines that taste more like grape juice than any other – but the high sugar levels ensure they are also among the most alcoholic of wines, too. Known as Moscato in Italy, the grape is much used for making sweet sparkling wines, as in Asti Spumante or Moscato d'Asti. There are several appellations in south-west France for inexpensive Muscats made rather like port, part-fermented before the addition of grape alcohol to halt the conversion of sugar into alcohol, creating a sweet and heady *vin doux naturel*. Dry Muscat wines, when well made, have a delicious sweet aroma but a refreshing, light touch with flavours reminiscent variously of orange blossom, wood smoke and grapefruit.

must – New-pressed grape juice prior to fermentation.

N

Navarra – DO wine-producing region of northern Spain adjacent to, and overshadowed by, Rioja. Navarra's wines can be startlingly akin to their neighbouring rivals, and sometimes rather better value for money.

négociant – In France, a dealer-producer who buys wines from growers and matures and/or blends them for bottling and sale under his or her own label. Purists can be a bit sniffy about these entrepreneurs, claiming that only the vine-grower with his or her own winemaking set-up can make truly authentic stuff, but the truth is that many of the best wines of France are *négociant*-produced – especially at the humbler end of the price scale. *Négociants* are often identified on wine labels as *négociant-éleveur* (literally 'dealer-bringer-up'), meaning that the wine has been matured, blended and bottled by the party in question.

Negroamaro – Black grape variety mainly of Puglia, the much-lauded wine region of south-east Italy. Dense, earthy red wines with ageing potential and plenty of alcohol. The name is probably (if not obviously) derived from Italian *negro* (black) and *amaro* (bitter). The grape behind Copertino, Salice Salentino and Squinzano.

Nerello Mascalese – Black grape of Sicily, most prolific in vineyards surrounding Mount Etna, making distinctive, flavoursome reds.

Nero d'Avola – Black grape variety of Sicily (Avola is a town in the province of Syracuse) and southern Italy. It makes deep-coloured wines that, given half a chance, can develop intensity and richness with age.

non-vintage – A wine is described as such when it has been blended from the harvests of more than one year. A non-vintage wine is not necessarily an inferior one, but under quality-control regulations around the world, still table wines most usually derive solely from one year's grape crop to qualify for appellation status. Champagnes and sparkling wines are mostly blended from several vintages, as are fortified wines such as port and sherry.

nose – In the vocabulary of the wine-taster, the nose is the scent of a wine. Sounds a bit dotty, but it makes a sensible enough alternative to the rather bald 'smell'. The use of the word 'perfume' implies that the wine smells particularly good. 'Aroma' is used specifically to describe a wine that smells as it should, as in 'this burgundy has the authentic strawberry-raspberry aroma of Pinot Noir'.

O

oak – Most of the world's costliest wines are matured in new or nearly new oak barrels, giving additional opulence of flavour. Of late, many cheaper wines have been getting the oak treatment, too, in older, cheaper casks, or simply by having sacks of oak chippings poured into their steel or fibreglass holding tanks. 'Oak aged' on a label is likely to indicate the latter treatments. But the overtly oaked wines of Australia have in some cases been so overdone that there is now a reactive trend whereby some producers proclaim their wines – particularly Chardonnays – as 'unoaked' on the label, thereby asserting that the flavours are more naturally achieved.

Oltrepo Pavese – Wine-producing zone of Piedmont, north-west Italy. The name means 'south of Pavia across the [river] Po' and the wines, both white and red, can be excellent quality and value for money.

organic wine – As in other sectors of the food industry, demand for organically made wine is – or appears to be – growing. As a rule, a wine qualifies as organic if it comes entirely from grapes grown in vineyards cultivated without the use of synthetic materials, and made in a winery where chemical treatments or additives are shunned with similar vigour. In fact, there are plenty of winemakers in the world using organic methods, but who disdain to label their bottles as such. Wines proclaiming their organic status used to carry the same sort of premium as their counterparts round the corner in the fruit, vegetable and meat aisles. But organic viticulture is now commonplace and there seems little price impact. There is no single worldwide (or even Europe-wide) standard for organic food or wine, so you pretty much have to take the producer's word for it.

P

Pasqua – One of the biggest and, it should be said, best wine producers of the Veneto region of north-west Italy.

Passerina – White grape variety of Marche, Italy. Used in blending but there is also a regional Passerina DOC.

Passetoutgrains – Designation for wine made from more than one grape variety grown in the same vineyard. French. Mostly red burgundy from Gamay and Pinot Noir.

Pays d'Oc – Shortened form under recent rule changes of French wine designation Vin de Pays d'Oc. All other similar regional designations can be similarly abbreviated.

Pecorino – White grape variety of mid-eastern Italy currently in vogue for well-coloured dry white varietal wines.

Periquita – Black grape variety of southern Portugal. Makes rather exotic spicy reds. Name means 'parrot'.

Perricone – Black grape variety of Sicily. Low-acid red wines.

PET – It's what they call plastic wine bottles – lighter to transport and allegedly as ecological as glass. Polyethylene terephthalate.

Petit Verdot – Black grape variety of Bordeaux contributing additional colour, density and spiciness to Cabernet Sauvignon-dominated blends. Mostly a minority player at home, but in Australia and California it is grown as the principal variety for some big hearty reds of real character.

petrol – When white wines from certain grapes, especially Riesling, are allowed to age in the bottle for longer than a year or two, they can take on a spirity aroma reminiscent of petrol or diesel. In grand mature German wines, this is considered a good thing.

Picpoul – Grape variety of southern France. Best known in Picpoul de Pinet, a dry white from near Sète on the Golfe de Lyon, lately elevated to AOP status. The name Picpoul (also Piquepoul) means 'stings the lips' – referring to the natural high acidity of the juice.

Piemonte – North-western province of Italy, which we call Piedmont, known for the spumante wines of the town of Asti, plus expensive Barbaresco and Barolo and better-value varietal red wines from Nebbiolo, Barbera and Dolcetto grapes.

Pinotage – South Africa's own black grape variety. Makes red wines ranging from light and juicy to dark, strong and long-lived. It's a cross between Pinot Noir and a grape the South Africans used to call Hermitage (thus the portmanteau name) but turns out to have been Cinsault.

Pinot Blanc – White grape variety principally of Alsace, France. Florally perfumed, exotically fruity dry white wines.

Pinot Grigio – White grape variety of northern Italy. Wines bearing its name are perplexingly fashionable. Good examples have an interesting smoky-pungent aroma and keen, slaking fruit. But most are dull. Originally French, it is at its best in the lushly exotic Pinot Gris wines of Alsace and is also successfully cultivated in Germany and New Zealand.

Pinot Noir – The great black grape of Burgundy, France. It makes all the region's fabulously expensive red wines. Notoriously difficult to grow in warmer climates, it is nevertheless cultivated by countless intrepid winemakers in the New World intent on reproducing the magic appeal of red burgundy. California and New Zealand have come closest. Some Chilean Pinot Noirs are inexpensive and worth trying.

Pouilly Fuissé – Village and AC of the Mâconnais region of southern Burgundy in France. Dry white wines from Chardonnay grapes. Wines are among the highest rated of the Mâconnais.

Pouilly Fumé – Village and AC of the Loire Valley in France. Dry white wines from Sauvignon Blanc grapes. Similar 'pebbly', 'grassy' or 'gooseberry' style to neighbouring AC Sancerre. The notion put about by some enthusiasts that Pouilly Fumé is 'smoky' is surely nothing more than word association with the name.

Primitivo – Black grape variety of southern Italy, especially the region of Puglia. Named from Latin *primus* for first, the grape is among the earliest-ripening of all varieties. The wines are typically dense and dark in colour with plenty of alcohol, and have an earthy, spicy style.

Priorat – Emerging wine region of Catalonia, Spain. Highly valued red wines from Garnacha and other varieties. Generic brands available in supermarkets are well worth trying out.

Prosecco – Softly sparkling wine of Italy's Veneto region. The best come from the DOCG Conegliano-Valdobbiadene, made as spumante ('foaming') wines in pressurised tanks, typically to 11 per cent alcohol and ranging from softly sweet to crisply dry. The constituent grape, previously also known as Prosecco, has been officially assigned the name Glera.

Puglia – The region occupying the 'heel' of southern Italy, making many good, inexpensive wines from indigenous grape varieties.

Q

QbA – German, standing for Qualitätswein bestimmter Anbaugebiete. It means 'quality wine from designated areas' and implies that the wine is made from grapes with a minimum level of ripeness, but it's by no means a guarantee of exciting quality. Only wines labelled QmP (see next entry) can be depended upon to be special.

QmP – Stands for Qualitätswein mit Prädikat. These are the serious wines of Germany, made without the addition of sugar to 'improve' them. To qualify for QmP status, the grapes must reach a level of ripeness as measured on a sweetness scale – all according to Germany's fiendishly complicated wine-quality regulations. Wines from grapes that reach the stated minimum level of sweetness qualify for the description of Kabinett. The next level up earns the rank of Spätlese, meaning 'late-picked'. Kabinett wines can be expected to be dry and brisk in style, and Spätlese wines a little bit riper and fuller. The next grade up, Auslese, meaning 'selected harvest', indicates a wine made from super-ripe grapes; it will be golden in colour and honeyed in flavour. A generation ago, these wines were as valued, and as expensive, as any of the world's grandest appellations. Beerenauslese and Trockenbeerenauslese are speciality wines made from individually picked late-harvest grapes.

Quincy – AC of Loire Valley, France, known for pebbly-dry white wines from Sauvignon grapes. The wines are forever compared to those of nearby and much better-known Sancerre – and Quincy often represents better value for money. Pronounced 'KAN-see'.

Quinta – Portuguese for farm or estate. It precedes the names of many of Portugal's best-known wines. It is pronounced 'KEEN-ta'.

R

racy – Evocative wine-tasting description for wine that thrills the tastebuds with a rush of exciting sensations. Good Rieslings often qualify.

raisiny – Wines from grapes that have been very ripe or overripe at harvest can take on a smell and flavour akin to the concentrated, heat-dried sweetness of raisins. As a minor element in the character of a wine, this can add to the appeal but as a dominant characteristic it is a fault.

rancio – Spanish term harking back to Roman times when wines were commonly stored in jars outside, exposed to the sun, so they oxidised and took on a burnt sort of flavour. Today, *rancio* describes a baked – and by no means unpleasant – flavour in fortified wines, particularly sherry and Madeira.

Reserva – In Portugal and Spain, this has genuine significance. The Portuguese use it for special wines with a higher alcohol level and longer ageing, although the precise periods vary between regions. In Spain, especially in the Navarra and Rioja regions, it means the wine must have had at least a year in oak and two in bottle before release.

reserve – On French (as *réserve*) or other wines, this implies special-quality, longer-aged wines, but has no official significance.

residual sugar – There is sugar in all wine, left over from the fermentation process. Some producers now mention the quantity of residual sugar on back labels in grams per litre of wine, even though so far there is no legal obligation to do so. Dry wines, red or white, typically have 3 g/l or fewer.

Above that, you might well be able to taste the sweetness. In southern hemisphere wines, made from grapes that have ripened under more-intense sunlight than their European counterparts, sugar levels can be correspondingly higher. Sweet wines such as Sauternes contain up to 150 g/l. Dry ('brut') sparkling wines made by the 'champagne' method typically have 10 g/l and tank-method fizzes such as prosecco up to 15 g/l.

Retsina – The universal white wine of Greece. It has been traditionally made in Attica, the region of Athens, for a very long time, and is said to owe its origins and name to the ancient custom of sealing amphorae (terracotta jars) of the wine with a gum made from pine resin. Some of the flavour of the resin inevitably transmitted itself into the wine, and ancient Greeks acquired a lasting taste for it.

Reuilly – AC of Loire Valley, France, for crisp dry whites from Sauvignon grapes. Pronounced 'RER-yee'.

Ribatejo – Emerging wine region of Portugal. Worth seeking out on labels of red wines in particular, because new winemakers are producing lively stuff from distinctive indigenous grapes such as Castelao and Trincadeira.

Ribera del Duero – Classic wine region of north-west Spain lying along the River Duero (which crosses the border to become Portugal's Douro, forming the valley where port comes from). It is home to an estate oddly named Vega Sicilia, where red wines of epic quality are made and sold at equally epic prices. Further down the scale, some very good reds are made, too.

Riesling – The noble grape variety of Germany. It is correctly pronounced 'REEZ-ling', not 'RICE-ling'. Once notorious as the grape behind all those boring 'medium' Liebfraumilches and Niersteiners, this grape has had a bad press. In fact, there has never been much, if any, Riesling in German plonk. But the country's best wines, the so-called Qualitätswein mit Prädikat grades, are made almost exclusively with Riesling. These wines range from crisply fresh and appley styles to extravagantly fruity, honeyed wines from late-harvested grapes. Excellent Riesling wines are also made in Alsace and now in Australasia.

Rioja – The principal fine-wine region of Spain, in the country's north east. The pricier wines are noted for their vanilla-pod richness from long ageing in oak casks. Tempranillo and Garnacha grapes make the reds, Viura the whites.

Ripasso – A particular style of Valpolicella wine. New wine is partially refermented in vats that have been used to make Recioto reds (wines made from semi-dried grapes), thus creating a bigger, smoother version of usually light and pale Valpolicella.

Riserva – In Italy, a wine made only in the best vintages, and allowed longer ageing in cask and bottle.

Rivaner – Alternative name for Germany's Müller-Thurgau grape.

Riverland – Vineyard region to the immediate north of the Barossa Valley of South Australia, extending east into New South Wales.

Roditis – White grape variety of Greece, known for fresh dry whites with decent acidity, often included in retsina.

rosso – Red wine, Italy.

Rosso Conero – DOC red wine made in the environs of Ancona in the Marches, Italy. Made from the Montepulciano grape, the wine can provide excellent value for money.

Ruby Cabernet – Black grape variety of California, created by crossing Cabernet Sauvignon and Carignan. Makes soft and squelchy red wine at home and in South Africa.

Rueda – DO of north-west Spain making first-class refreshing dry whites from the indigenous Verdejo grape, imported Sauvignon, and others. Exciting quality, and prices are keen.

Rully – AC of Chalonnais region of southern Burgundy, France. White wines from Chardonnay and red wines from Pinot Noir grapes. Both can be very good and substantially cheaper than their more northerly Burgundian neighbours. Pronounced 'ROO-yee'.

S

Sagrantino – Black grape variety native to Perugia, Italy. Dark, tannic wines best known in DOCG Sagrantino de Montefalco. Now also cultivated in Australia.

Saint Emilion – AC of Bordeaux, France. Centred on the romantic hill town of St Emilion, this famous sub-region makes some of the grandest red wines of France, but also some of the best-value ones. Less fashionable than the Médoc region on the opposite (west) bank of the River Gironde that bisects Bordeaux, St Emilion wines are made largely with the Merlot grape, and are relatively quick to mature. The top wines are classified *1er grand cru classé* and are madly expensive, but many more are classified respectively *grand cru classé* and *grand cru*, and these designations can be seen as a fairly trustworthy indicator of quality. There are several 'satellite' St Emilion ACs named after the villages at their centres, notably Lussac St Emilion, Montagne St Emilion and Puisseguin St Emilion. Some excellent wines are made by estates within these ACs, and at relatively affordable prices thanks to the comparatively humble status of their satellite designations.

Salento – Up-and-coming wine region of southern Italy. Many good bargain reds from local grapes including Nero d'Avola and Primitivo.

Sancerre – AC of the Loire Valley, France, renowned for flinty-fresh Sauvignon Blanc whites and rarer Pinot Noir reds and rosés.

Sangiovese – The local black grape of Tuscany, Italy, is the principal variety used for Chianti. Also planted further south in Italy and in the New World.

Generic Sangiovese di Toscana can make a consoling substitute for costly Chianti.

Saumur – Town and appellation of Loire Valley, France. Characterful minerally red wines from Cabernet Franc grapes, and some whites. Sparkling wines from Chenin Blanc grapes can be good value.

Saumur-Champigny – Separate appellation for red wines from Cabernet Franc grapes of Saumur in the Loire, sometimes very good and lively.

Sauvignon Blanc – French white grape variety now grown worldwide. New Zealand has raised worldwide production values challenging the long supremacy of French ACs in Bordeaux and the Loire Valley. Chile and South Africa aspire similarly. The wines are characterised by aromas of gooseberry, peapod, fresh-cut grass, even asparagus. Flavours are often described as 'grassy' or 'nettly'.

sec – Dry wine style. French.

secco – Dry wine style. Italian.

seco – Dry wine style. Spanish.

Semillon – White grape variety originally of Bordeaux, where it is blended with Sauvignon Blanc to make fresh dry whites and, when harvested very late in the season, the ambrosial sweet whites of Barsac, Sauternes and other appellations. Even in the driest wines, the grape can be recognised from its honeyed, sweet-pineapple, even banana-like aromas. Now widely planted in Australia and Latin America, and frequently blended with Chardonnay to make dry whites, some of them interesting.

sherry – The great aperitif wine of Spain, centred on the Andalusian city of Jerez (the name 'sherry' is an English mispronunciation). There is a lot of sherry-style wine in the world, but only the authentic wine from Jerez and the neighbouring producing centres of Puerta de Santa Maria and Sanlucar de Barrameda may label their wines as such. The Spanish drink real sherry – very dry and fresh, pale in colour and served well-chilled – called fino and manzanilla, and darker but naturally dry variations called amontillado, palo cortado and oloroso.

Shiraz – Australian name for the Syrah grape. The variety is the most widely planted of any in Australia, and makes red wines of wildly varying quality, characterised by dense colour, high alcohol, spicy fruit and generous, cushiony texture.

Somontano – Wine region of north-east Spain. Name means 'under the mountains' – in this case the Pyrenees – and the region has had DO status since 1984. Much innovative winemaking here, with New World styles emerging. Some very good buys. A region to watch.

souple – French wine-tasting term that translates into English as 'supple' or even 'docile' as in 'pliable', but I understand it in the vinous context to mean muscular but soft – a wine with tannin as well as soft fruit.

Spätlese – *See* QmP.

spirity – Some wines, mostly from the New World, are made from grapes so ripe at harvest that their high alcohol content can be detected through a mildly burning sensation on the tongue, similar to the effect of sipping a spirit. Young Port wines can be detectably spirity.

spritzy – Describes a wine with a gentle sparkle. Some young wines are intended to have this elusive fizziness; in others it is a fault.

spumante – Sparkling wine of Italy. Asti Spumante is the best known, from the town of Asti in the north-west Italian province of Piemonte. Many Prosecco wines are labelled as Spumante in style. The term describes wines that are fully sparkling. Frizzante wines have a less vigorous mousse.

stalky – A useful tasting term to describe red wines with flavours that make you think the stalks from the grape bunches must have been fermented along with the must (juice). Red Loire wines and youthful claret very often have this mild astringency. In moderation it's fine, but if it dominates it probably signifies the wine is at best immature and at worst badly made.

Stellenbosch – Town and region at the heart of South Africa's wine industry. It's an hour's drive from Cape Town and the source of much of the country's cheaper wine. Some serious-quality estate wines as well.

stony – Wine-tasting term for keenly dry white wines. It's meant to indicate a wine of purity and real quality, with just the right match of fruit and acidity.

structured – Good wines are not one-dimensional, they have layers of flavour and texture. A structured wine has phases of enjoyment: the 'attack', or first impression in the mouth; the middle palate as the wine is held in the mouth; and the lingering aftertaste.

sugar – *See* residual sugar.

sulphites – Nearly all wines, barring some esoteric 'natural' types of a kind not found in supermarkets are made with the aid of preparations containing sulphur to combat diseases in the vineyards and bacterial infections in the winery. It's difficult to make wine without sulphur. Even 'organic' wines need it. Because some people are sensitive to the traces of sulphur in some wines, worldwide health authorities insist wine labels bear the warning 'Contains sulphites'.

summer fruit – Wine-tasting term intended to convey a smell or taste of soft fruits such as strawberries and raspberries – without having to commit too specifically to which.

superiore – On labels of Italian wines, this is more than an idle boast. Under DOC(G) rules, wines must qualify for the *superiore* designation by reaching one or more specified quality levels, usually a higher alcohol content or an additional period of maturation. Frascati, for example, qualifies for DOC status at 11.5 per cent alcohol, but to be classified *superiore* must have 12 per cent alcohol.

sur lie – Literally, 'on the lees'. It's a term now widely used on the labels of Muscadet wines, signifying that after fermentation has died down, the new wine has been left in the tank over the winter on the lees – the detritus of yeasts and other interesting compounds left over from the turbid fermentation process. The idea is that additional interest is imparted into the flavour of the wine.

Syrah – The noble grape of the Rhône Valley, France. Makes very dark, dense wine characterised by peppery, tarry aromas. Now planted all over southern France and farther afield. In Australia it is known as Shiraz.

T

table wine – Wine that is unfortified and of an alcoholic strength, for UK tax purposes anyway, of no more than 15 per cent. I use the term to distinguish, for example, between the red table wines of the Douro Valley in Portugal and the region's better-known fortified wine, port.

Tafelwein – Table wine, German. The humblest quality designation, which doesn't usually bode very well.

tank method – Bulk-production process for sparkling wines. Base wine undergoes secondary fermentation in a large, sealed vat rather than in individual closed bottles. Also known as the Charmat method after the name of the inventor of the process. Prosecco is made by the tank method.

Tai – White grape variety of north-east Italy, a relative of Sauvignon Blanc. Also known in Italy as Tocai Friulano or, more correctly, Friulano.

Tannat – Black grape of south-west France, notably for wines of Madiran, and lately named as the variety most beneficial to health thanks to its outstanding antioxidant content.

tannin – Well known as the film-forming, teeth-coating component in tea, tannin is a natural compound that occurs in black grape skins and acts as a natural preservative in wine. Its noticeable presence in wine is regarded as a good thing. It gives young everyday reds their dryness, firmness of flavour and backbone. And it helps high-quality reds to retain their lively fruitiness for many years. A grand Bordeaux red when first made, for example, will have purply-sweet, rich fruit and mouth-puckering tannin, but after ten years or so this will have evolved into a delectably fruity, mature wine in which the formerly parching effects of the tannin have receded almost completely, leaving the shade of 'residual tannin' that marks out a great wine approaching maturity.

Tarrango – Black grape variety of Australia.

tarry – On the whole, winemakers don't like critics to say their wines evoke the redolence of road repairs, but I can't help using this term to describe the agreeable, sweet, 'burnt' flavour that is often found at the centre of the fruit in red wines from Argentina, Italy, Portugal and South Africa in particular.

TCA – Dreaded ailment in wine, usually blamed on faulty corks. It stands for 246 *trichloroanisol* and is characterised by a horrible musty smell and flavour in the affected wine. Thanks to technological advances made by cork manufacturers in Portugal – the leading cork nation – TCA is now in retreat.

tears – The colourless alcohol in the wine left clinging to the inside of the glass after the contents have been swirled. Persistent tears (also known as 'legs') indicate a wine of good concentration.

Tempranillo – The great black grape of Spain. Along with Garnacha (Grenache in France) it makes most red Rioja and Navarra wines and, under many pseudonyms, is an important or exclusive contributor to the wines of many other regions of Spain. It is also widely cultivated in South America.

Teroldego – Black grape variety of Trentino, northern Italy. Often known as Teroldego Rotaliano after the Rotaliano region where most of the vineyards lie. Deep-coloured, assertive, green-edged red wines.

terroir – French word for 'ground' or 'soil' has mystical meaning in vineyard country. Winemakers attribute the distinct characteristics of their products, not just to the soil conditions but to the lie of the land and the prevailing (micro)climate, all within the realm of terroir. The word now frequently appears on effusive back labels asserting the unique appeal of the wine. Some critics scoff that terroir is all imagined nonsense.

tinto – On Spanish labels indicates a deeply coloured red wine. Clarete denotes a paler colour. Also Portuguese.

Toro – Quality wine region east of Zamora, Spain.

Torrontes – White grape variety of Argentina. Makes soft, dry wines often with delicious grapey-spicy aroma, similar in style to the classic dry Muscat wines of Alsace, but at more accessible prices.

Touraine – Region encompassing a swathe of the Loire Valley, France. Non-AC wines may be labelled 'Sauvignon de Touraine'.

Touriga Nacional – The most valued black grape variety of the Douro Valley in Portugal, where port is made. The name Touriga now appears on an increasing number of table wines made as sidelines by the port producers. They can be very good, with the same spirity aroma and sleek flavours of port itself, minus the fortification.

Traminer – Grape variety, the same as Gewürztraminer.

Trebbiano – The workhorse white grape of Italy. A productive variety that is easy to cultivate, it seems to be included in just about every ordinary white wine of the entire nation – including Frascati, Orvieto and Soave. It is the same grape as France's Ugni Blanc. There are, however, distinct regional variations of the grape. Trebbiano di Lugana (also known as Turbiana) makes a distinctive white in the DOC of the name, sometimes very good, while Trebbiano di Toscana makes a major contribution to the distinctly less interesting dry whites of Chianti country.

Trincadeira Preta – Portuguese black grape variety native to the port-producing vineyards of the Douro Valley (where it goes under the name Tinta Amarella). In southern Portugal, it produces dark and sturdy table wines.

trocken – 'Dry' German wine. The description does have a particular meaning under German wine law, namely that there is only a low level of unfermented sugar lingering in the wine (9 grams per litre, if you need to know), and this can leave the wine tasting rather austere.

U

Ugni Blanc – The most widely cultivated white grape variety of France and the mainstay of many a cheap dry white wine. To date it has been better known as the provider of base wine for distilling into armagnac and cognac, but lately the name has been appearing on wine labels. Technology seems to be improving the performance of the grape. The curious name is pronounced 'OON-yee', and is the same variety as Italy's ubiquitous Trebbiano.

Utiel-Requena – Region and *Denominación de Origen* of Mediterranean Spain inland from Valencia. Principally red wines from Bobal, Garnacha and Tempranillo grapes grown at relatively high altitude, between 600 and 900 metres.

V

Vacqueyras – Village of the southern Rhône Valley of France in the region better known for its generic appellation, the Côtes du Rhône. Vacqueyras can date its winemaking history all the way back to 1414, but has only been producing under its own village AC since 1991. The wines, from Grenache and Syrah grapes, can be wonderfully silky and intense, spicy and long-lived.

Valdepeñas – An island of quality production amidst the ocean of mediocrity that is Spain's La Mancha region – where most of the grapes are grown for distilling into the head-banging brandies of Jerez. Valdepeñas reds are made from a grape they call the Cencibel – which turns out to be a very close relation of the Tempranillo grape that is the mainstay of the fine but expensive red wines of Rioja. Again, like Rioja, Valdepeñas wines are matured in oak casks to give them a vanilla-rich smoothness. Among bargain reds, Valdepeñas is a name to look out for.

Valpolicella – Red wine of Verona, Italy. Good examples have ripe, cherry fruit and a pleasingly dry finish. Unfortunately, there are many bad examples of Valpolicella. Shop with circumspection. Valpolicella Classico wines, from the best vineyards clustered around the town, are more reliable.

Those additionally labelled *superiore* have higher alcohol and some bottle age.

vanilla – Ageing wines in oak barrels (or, less picturesquely, adding oak chips to wine in huge concrete vats) imparts a range of characteristics including a smell of vanilla from the ethyl vanilline naturally given off by oak.

varietal – A varietal wine is one named after the grape variety (one or more) from which it is made. Nearly all everyday wines worldwide are now labelled in this way. It is salutary to contemplate that until the present wine boom began in the 1980s, wines described thus were virtually unknown outside Germany and one or two quirky regions of France and Italy.

vegan-friendly – My informal way of noting that a wine is claimed to have been made not only with animal-product-free finings (*see* vegetarian wine) but without any animal-related products whatsoever, such as livestock manure in the vineyards.

vegetal – A tasting note definitely open to interpretation. It suggests a smell or flavour reminiscent less of fruit (apple, pineapple, strawberry and the like) than of something leafy or even root based. Some wines are evocative (to some tastes) of beetroot, cabbage or even unlikelier vegetable flavours – and these characteristics may add materially to the attraction of the wine.

vegetarian wine – Wines labelled 'suitable for vegetarians' have been made without the assistance of animal products for 'fining' – clarifying – before bottling. Gelatine, egg whites, isinglass from fish bladders and casein from milk are among the items shunned, usually in favour of bentonite, an absorbent clay first found at Benton in the US state of Montana.

Verdejo – White grape of the Rueda region in north-west Spain. It can make superbly perfumed crisp dry whites of truly distinctive character and has helped make Rueda one of the best white-wine sources of Europe. No relation to Verdelho.

Verdelho – Portuguese grape variety once mainly used for a medium-dry style of Madeira, also called Verdelho, but now rare. The vine is now prospering in Australia, where it can make well-balanced dry whites with fleeting richness and lemon-lime acidity.

Verdicchio – White grape variety of Italy best known in the DOC zone of Castelli di Jesi in the Adriatic wine region of the Marches. Dry white wines once known for little more than their naff amphora-style bottles but now gaining a reputation for interesting, herbaceous flavours of recognisable character.

Vermentino – White grape variety principally of Italy, especially Sardinia. Makes florally scented soft dry whites.

Vieilles vignes – Old vines. Many French producers like to claim on their labels that the wine within is from vines of notable antiquity. While it's true that vines don't produce useful grapes for the first few years after planting, it is uncertain whether vines of much greater age – say 25 years plus – than others actually make better fruit. There are no regulations governing the use of the term, so it's not a reliable indicator anyway.

Vin de France – In effect, the new Vin de Table of France's morphing wine laws. The label may state the vintage (if all the wine in the blend does come from a single year's harvest) and the grape varieties that constitute the wine. It may not state the region of France from which the wine originates.

vin de liqueur – Sweet style of white wine mostly from the Pyrenean region of south-westernmost France, made by adding a little spirit to the new wine before it has fermented out, halting the fermentation and retaining sugar.

vin de pays – 'Country wine' of France. Introduced in 1968 and regularly revised ever since, it's the wine-quality designation between basic Vin de France and AOC/AOP. Although being superseded by the more recently introduced IGP (*qv*), there are more than 150 producing areas permitted to use the description vin de pays. Some vin de pays areas are huge: the Vin de Pays d'Oc (referencing the Languedoc region) covers much of the Midi and Provence. Plenty of wines bearing this humble designation are of astoundingly high quality and certainly compete with New World counterparts for interest and value. *See* Indication Géographique Protégée.

vin de table – Formerly official designation of generic French wine, now used only informally. *See* Vin de France.

vin doux naturel – Sweet, mildly fortified wine of southern France. A little spirit is added during the winemaking process, halting the fermentation by killing the yeast before it has consumed all the sugars – hence the pronounced sweetness of the wine.

vin gris – Rosé wine from Provence.

Vinho de mesa – 'Table wine' of Portugal.

Vino da tavola – The humblest official classification of Italian wine. Much ordinary plonk bears this designation, but the bizarre quirks of Italy's wine laws dictate that some of that country's finest wines are also classed as mere vino da tavola (table wine). If an expensive Italian wine is labelled as such, it doesn't mean it will be a disappointment.

Vino de la Tierra – Generic classification for regional wines, Spain. Abbreviates to VdT.

Vino de mesa – 'Table wine' of Spain. Usually very ordinary.

vintage – The grape harvest. The year displayed on bottle labels is the year of the harvest. Wines bearing no date have been blended from the harvests of two or more years.

Viognier – A white grape variety once exclusive to the northern Rhône Valley in France where it makes expensive Condrieu. Now, Viognier is grown more widely, in North and South America as well as elsewhere in France, and occasionally produces soft, marrowy whites that echo the grand style of Condrieu itself. The Viognier is now commonly blended with

Shiraz in red winemaking in Australia and South Africa. It does not dilute the colour and is confidently believed by highly experienced winemakers to enhance the quality. Steve Webber, in charge of winemaking at the revered De Bortoli estates in the Yarra Valley region of Victoria, Australia, puts between two and five per cent Viognier in with some of his Shiraz wines. 'I think it's the perfume,' he told me. 'It gives some femininity to the wine.'

Viura – White grape variety of Rioja, Spain. Also widely grown elsewhere in Spain under the name Macabeo. Wines have a blossomy aroma and are dry, but sometimes soft at the expense of acidity.

Vouvray – AC of the Loire Valley, France, known for still and sparkling dry white wines and sweet, still whites from late-harvested grapes. The wines, all from Chenin Blanc grapes, have a unique capacity for unctuous softness combined with lively freshness – an effect best portrayed in the demi-sec (slightly sweet) wines, which can be delicious and keenly priced.

Vranac – Black grape variety of the Balkans known for dense colour and tangy-bitter edge to the flavour. Best enjoyed in situ.

W

weight – In an ideal world the weight of a wine is determined by the ripeness of the grapes from which it has been made. In some cases the weight is determined merely by the quantity of sugar added during the production process. A good, genuine wine described as having weight is one in which there is plenty of alcohol and 'extract' – colour and flavour from the grapes. Wine enthusiasts judge weight by swirling the wine in the glass and then examining the 'legs' or 'tears' left clinging to the inside of the glass after the contents have subsided. Alcohol gives these runlets a dense, glycerine-like condition, and if they cling for a long time, the wine is deemed to have weight – a very good thing in all honestly made wines.

Winzergenossenschaft – One of the many very lengthy and peculiar words regularly found on labels of German wines. This means a winemaking co-operative. Many excellent German wines are made by these associations of growers.

woody – A subjective tasting note. A faintly rank odour or flavour suggesting the wine has spent too long in cask.

X

Xarel-lo – One of the main grape varieties for cava, the sparkling wine of Spain.

Xinomavro – Black grape variety of Greece. It retains its acidity even in the very hot conditions that prevail in many Greek vineyards, where harvests tend to over-ripen and make cooked-tasting wines. Modern winemaking techniques are capable of making well-balanced wines from Xinomavro.

Y

Yecla – Town and DO wine region of eastern Spain, close to Alicante, making interesting, strong-flavoured red and white wines, often at bargain prices.

yellow – White wines are not white at all, but various shades of yellow – or, more poetically, gold. Some white wines with opulent richness even have a flavour I cannot resist calling yellow – reminiscent of butter.

Z

Zibibbo – Sicilian white grape variety synonymous with north African variety Muscat of Alexandria. Scantily employed in sweet winemaking, and occasionally for drier styles.

Zierfandler – Esoteric white grape of Thermenregion, Austria. Aromatic dry wines and rare late-harvest sweet wines.

Zinfandel – Black grape variety of California. Makes brambly reds, some of which can age very gracefully, and 'blush' whites – actually pink, because a little of the skin colour is allowed to leach into the must. The vine is also planted in Australia and South America. The Primitivo of southern Italy is said to be a related variety, but makes a very different kind of wine.

Zweigelt – Black grape of Austria making juicy red wines for drinking young. Some wines are aged in oak to make interesting, heftier long-keepers.

Index